Freddy & Gwen
COLLABORATE
AGAIN

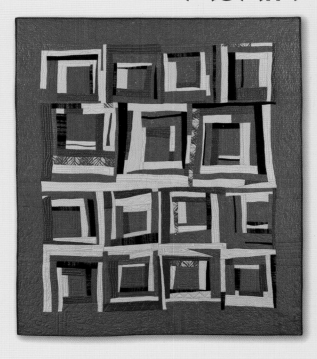

Freddy & Gwen
COLLABORATE AGAIN

Freewheeling Twists on Traditional Quilt Designs

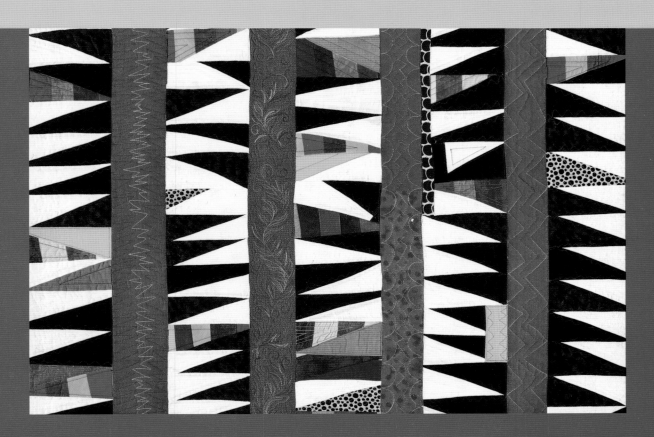

GWEN·MARSTON & FREDDY MORAN

LARK BOOKS

A Division of Sterling Publishing Co., Inc.
New York / London

Red Lips 4 Courage Communications, Inc.

www.redlips4courage.com

Eileen Cannon Paulin
President

Catherine Risling
Director of Editorial

Senior Editor: Darra Williamson
Copy Editor: Catherine Risling
Art Director: Susan H. Hartman
Illustrator: Kim Coxey
Photographer: Gregory Case

Library of Congress Cataloging-in-Publication Data

Marston, Gwen.
 Freddy & Gwen Collaborate Again / Gwen Marston and Freddy Moran.
  p. cm.
 Includes bibliographical references and index.
 ISBN 978-1-60059-439-7 (pbk. : alk. paper)
 1. Quilting--Patterns. 2. Patchwork--Patterns. I. Moran, Freddy, 1930-
II. Title.
 TT835.M678353 2008
 746.46'041--dc22
                        2008034581

10 9 8 7 6 5 4 3 2

Published by Lark Books, A Division of
Sterling Publishing Co., Inc.
387 Park Ave. South, New York, NY 10016

Text © 2009, Gwen Marston and Freddy Moran
Photography © 2009, Red Lips 4 Courage Communications, Inc.
Illustrations © 2009, Red Lips 4 Courage Communications, Inc.

Distributed in Canada by Sterling Publishing,
c/o Canadian Manda Group, 165 Dufferin St.
Toronto, Ontario, Canada M6K 3H6

Distributed in the United Kingdom by GMC Distribution Services,
Castle Place, 166 High St., Lewes, East Sussex, England BN7 1XU

Distributed in Australia by Capricorn Link (Australia) Pty Ltd.,
P.O. Box 704, Windsor, NSW 2756 Australia

If you have questions or comments about this book, please contact:

Lark Books
67 Broadway
Asheville, NC 28801
(828) 253-0467

Manufactured in China

ISBN 13: 978-1-60059-439-7

For information about custom editions, special sales, premium and corporate purchases, please contact Sterling Special Sales Department at (800) 805-5489 or specialsales@sterlingpub.com.

Dedication

We dedicate this book to Neil Moran, who lovingly made us French roast coffee and supported us in every way. We also dedicate our second collaborative book to our children and our grandchildren, for their enduring encouragement and inspiration.

Contents

Introduction

$\mathscr{F}$ive years have passed since we began our collaboration, which resulted in four exhibits: MAQS Museum in Paducah, Kentucky; The LaConner Quilt Museum in LaConner, Washington; New Pieces in Berkeley, California; and The Back Porch in Pacific Grove, California. It also resulted in our first book together, *Collaborative Quilting* (see Bibliography, page 189), which shows glorious, full-page color photos of 60 of our individual quilts and 32 collaborative quilts, along with instructions for constructing the parts that make up each quilt. Quilters find this book easy to use because the quilts in the gallery and the instructions are cross-referenced. Every quilt is accompanied by a list of the parts used in the quilt, and the instructional section, called The Parts Department, lists all the quilts in which that particular part has been used.

In this, our second collaborative book, we introduce very different-looking quilts and the new parts that went into them. Once again, we include easy instructions for making the parts, and cross-reference them with the quilts. What is new and different in this second book is the focus on how we designed those quilts.

We share with you not only how to make all the parts, but how to use them to design *your own original quilt.* There is lots of focus, too, on where the inspiration comes from so the link between the old and new becomes very clear.

More and more, we see quilters who are technically capable, but less sure of themselves when it comes to creating original work ... and more and more quilters want to create their own work. Consider the fact that our quilting ancestors didn't have commercial patterns and frequently weren't formally educated, yet still managed to make wonderful quilts. If they could do it, so can we. Yes, we can!

Another difference in this second book is the quilts themselves. Our first book featured many quilts with small blocks. For *Freddy & Gwen Collaborate Again*, we worked with larger, bolder designs, and introduce five works in solids inspired by the strong graphic work for which African-American quilters are known. The quilts in this book rely more heavily on liberated methods to create quilts in an unstructured style, and less on traditional blocks.

So buckle up ... it's going to be an exciting and wonderful ride!

Gwen Marston

Freddy Moran

This is the cover quilt from our first book, *Collaborative Quilting.* As you'll see in the following pages, our creative collaboration continues to grow.

Chapter 1

Designing with Gwen: Lessons Learned from Antique Quilts

I fell in love with antique quilts three decades ago, and I am as enthusiastic about them as ever. Antique quilts continue to inspire and inform my own work. What I know about quiltmaking, I've learned from studying antique quilts. They are ripe with innovative ideas that can inspire and energize our own work.

Tradition as Inspiration

Artistically, I am drawn to antique quilts for their sense of spontaneity and originality. As late as 1930, the largest part of the American population lived on farms. Isolation meant that quilters had to rely upon themselves for artistic ideas and technical solutions. There wasn't the wide availability of commercial patterns we have today, nor were there books or quilt magazines arriving in the mail. Quilters had to figure things out for themselves and this resulted in a lot of diversity.

For example, you can find a lot of antique Rose Wreath appliqués, but you rarely find two that are identical.

Antique quilts often have a freshness and inventiveness that may come in part from the fact that they were less manipulated and controlled than is common today. Quilters in the past allowed asymmetry in block placement and borders. They accepted random placement of color. They didn't waste time over-engineering their quilts and I think that has a lot to do with the artistic success of the resulting work. Most great painters haven't lost sleep trying to stay inside the lines. Working more freely, more loosely, our quilting ancestors made quilts that spark the imagination and delight us with their inventiveness.

■ A Second Major Influence

Another major influence in my understanding of quilt design has been the work of African-American quilters. African-American quilters have been busy making quilts as long as Anglo-American quilters, but—for far too long—their work remained unknown, even among a large portion of the burgeoning quilt community.

I became aware of these quilters with the publication of an exhibit catalog, *The Afro-American Tradition in Decorative Arts* (see Bibliography, page 189), which included a sampling of exciting quilts unlike any I'd ever seen. Since then, quilt scholars such as the late Cuesta Benberry have brought these exciting quilts to the larger community through books, articles, and exhibits. Now, with the blockbuster exhibits and accompanying books introducing the quilters from Gee's Bend, Alabama, the work of African-Americans has been recognized by the art community *and* the quilt community. There are a number of collaborative quilts in this book that were influenced by African-American work.

■ Stop, Look … and Learn

In designing your own quilts, remember that you don't need to reinvent the wheel. You have hundreds of years of tradition available to you, both through books and museums. You can use traditional blocks and settings that belong to all of us. You can adapt artistic ideas from antique quilts in your own work. You can also use traditional techniques, some of which are frankly easier than modern methods. You can study antique quilts for color ideas. I studied old samplers (pages 14 and 15) for color ideas when I made my sampler quilts (pages 32 and 33).

I wanted to make quilts that had the same artistic elements as the old tops in my collection. Notice how I sewed the borders on without worrying about resolving the corners. I am very comfortable using unresolved borders, reminding myself (and hopefully the viewer) that I have years of tradition backing me up. I feel that making the corners work out precisely or letting them have free rein are equally suitable options.

■ Three Rich Examples

On the next three pages you'll find examples of antique quilts with lessons to teach us. These are three of many such quilts in my collection and all of them tell common stories about using simple shapes and allowing random events to occur spontaneously.

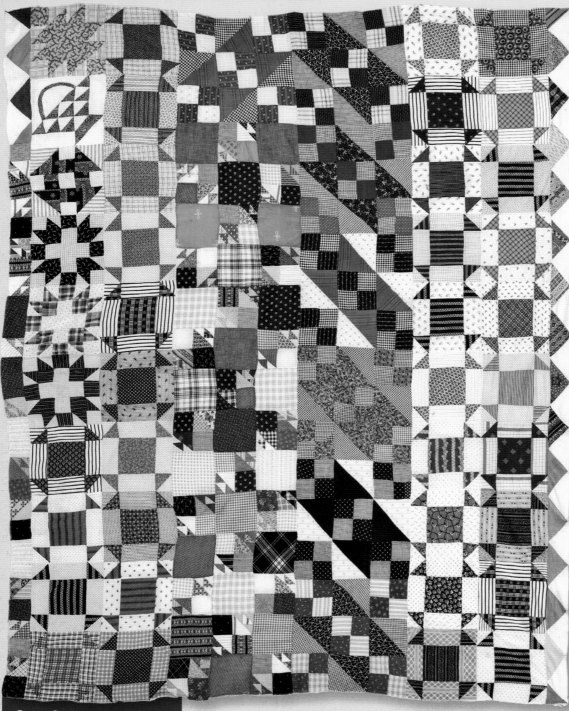

Sampler

(quilt top, c. 1890–1910)
72" × 92" (182.9 cm × 233.7 cm)
Collection of Gwen Marston

This is a typical antique sampler of the kind that has inspired our collaborative work. It's a fascinating collection of blocks set into rows that interact with the adjacent rows. There is a lot going on here and it doesn't get much better than this.

Notice the Sawtooth border that runs along one side with three of the units making it to the opposite side before being replaced with other units found in the body of the quilt. This is a quilt to study carefully.

Pennsylvania Sampler

(quilt top, c. 1890–1910)
65" × 70" (165.1 cm × 177.8 cm)
Collection of Gwen Marston

This is one of two samplers that had been sewn together to make a featherbed covering. Notice that there are simple blocks, as well as a few complex blocks. With a little study you can find the fillers used to make the blocks fit together. One example is the two Flying (or Wild) Geese and two squares sewn to the small green Variable Star block in the top row to make it fit the adjoining block.

Also notice that the blocks called Single Wedding Ring, Georgetown Circle, or Crown of Thorns (third row from the left) are hard to recognize as the same block due to the coloration of the blocks. Other areas of interest are created by three groups of dark-colored blocks placed arbitrarily in the quilt. These are little reminders that allowing random events to occur can make a quilt more interesting, and that too much coordination can wring all the energy right out of a quilt.

Four Patch

(c. 1910–1920)
68" × 79" (172.7 cm × 200.7 cm)
Made by Sarah Gruber Replagle,
Breezewood, Pennsylvania
Collection of Gwen Marston

Like this quilt, many antique quilts were made with simple blocks arranged in uncomplicated sets. Yet Sarah and many quilters of her era produced quilts with so many surprises in color and placement of patches that the quilts rise to a high level of design. Study the blocks to find the subtle variations Sarah worked into her quilt.

Here are some of the ways Sarah added interest and depth to her quilt.

- She made blocks using different prints of the same color.

- She turned the predominant color in the four patches in different directions, creating a completely different visual.

- She made blocks using red in both the large squares and the four patches so that the red parts of the four patches seem to disappear.

Sarah finished the edges by rolling the top over to the back and stitching it down. This was a common way to finish quilts in the past because you could use what was already there instead of cutting into new fabric to make a separate binding. Another common method was to bring the backing around to the front and stitch it down, often by topstitching it on the sewing machine. This is what we did on *Arbie's Quilt* (page 136), *Around the Block* (page 138), and *Marzella's Quilt* (page 166). Instructions for this simple technique appear on page 75.

Going for It

Designing quilts as you go, with pre-made parts, without planned outcomes, confidently resolving technical problems along the way, is a completely liberating way to approach the art of quiltmaking. One more tip on learning how to design your own work: Your chances for doing something innovative are enhanced when you start "playing around" and taking some chances. So be adventuresome! Be a little risky, have some fun, go out on a limb. That's where the fruit is.

I leave you with a story I was told when teaching a class on the western shore of Michigan some years ago:

Neva Banks was born in 1889 in Ravenna, Michigan. She had only a fourth-grade education. She never wore black, brown, grey, or navy. She was buried at a ripe old age in a bright red pantsuit. Neva never had enough fabric to make clothes, so she pieced the yokes and other parts of the dresses she made for herself. Explaining her tricks for working with insufficient fabric, Neva said, "You have to piece boldly."

Baskets with Dog Tooth Handles

72" × 72" (182.9 cm × 182.9 cm) ▪ 2007

Tradition . . .

This vintage block from my collection is a "kissing cousin" to the blocks in this quilt, and also inspired our collaborative quilt *Baskets with Sawtooth Handles* (page 140).

The idea for this quilt was inspired by a circa-1850 quilt, which appeared in *The Quilt Engagement Calendar 1992*. (See Bibliography, page 189.) What caught my eye were the Sawtooth handles, which I cut from folded fabric for a playful look. The idea for adding the eggs came from an antique block in my collection. Designed, made, and hand quilted by Gwen Marston.

Parts *Basket with Sawtooth Handle* (page 82)
Half-Square-Triangle Unit (page 94)

Betty and Maude's Baskets

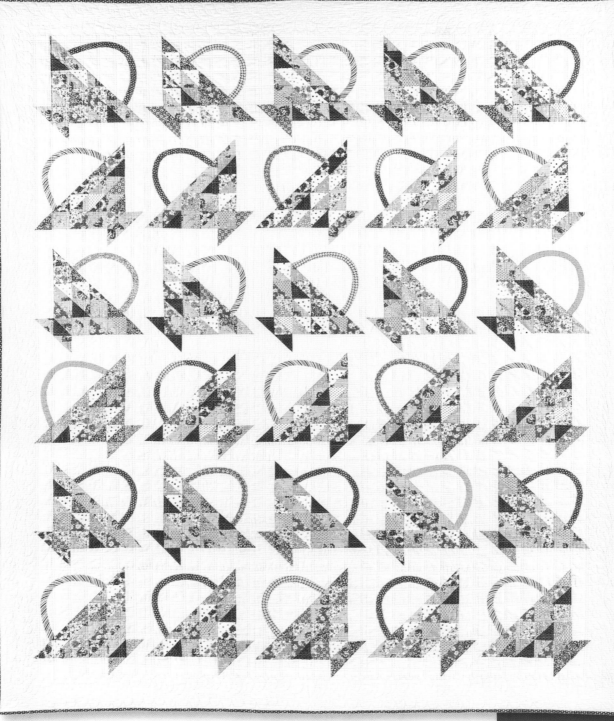

72" × 85" (182.9 cm × 215.9 cm) ▪ 2007

A wonderful collection of 1940s reproduction fabrics called "Betty and Maude" provided the inspiration for this quilt. Notice that some basket handles are pieced to include a second color, a fun idea I got from seeing it on an antique quilt. Designed and made by Gwen Marston; machine quilted by Robyn House.

71" × 78" (180.3 cm × 198.1 cm) ▪ 1995

The reverse side of this quilt is as good as the front. The plain field of color makes a great canvas for showcasing the sumptuousness of the Welsh-inspired quilting designs.

I appliquéd the center of this quilt in 1988, but it wasn't completed until 1995 as a gift for my son, Matthew. Hidden in the quilting are Matthew's name, the word "Mom," and two hearts. The centipede design came from a Middle Eastern rug in my home, and I adapted traditional Welsh quilting designs to cover the surface. Designed, made, and hand quilted by Gwen Marston.

Parts   *Strata* (page 125)

Chinese Coins and Sixteen Patches

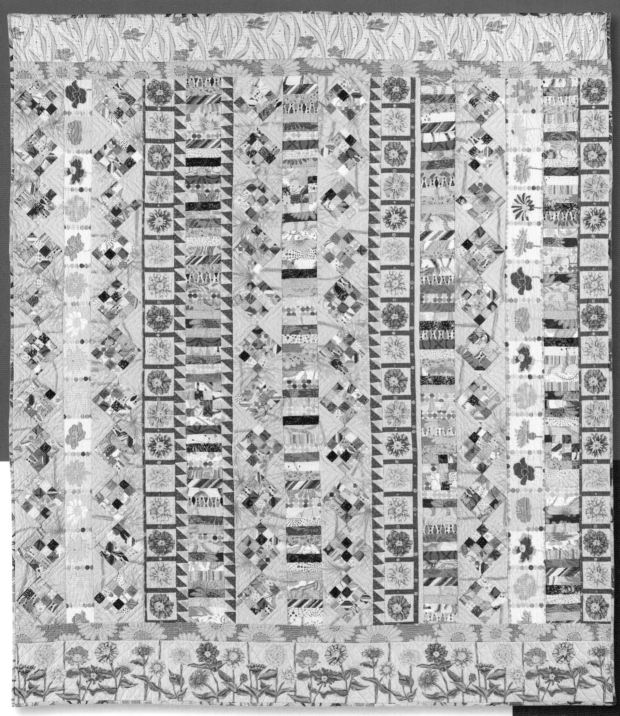

60" × 70"
(152.4 cm × 177.8 cm)
2006

This quilt is a good example of how you can use simple blocks to make a successful quilt and of finding fabric (in this case, designed by Valori Wells) that can do a lot of the work for you. The flowered strips are not pieced, but rather came printed that way, as did the row of zinnias along the bottom edge. Designed and made by Gwen Marston; machine quilted by Robyn House.

Parts   *Half-Square-Triangle Unit* (page 94)
Strata (page 125)

Chintz Medallion

62" × 62" (157.5 cm × 157.5 cm) ▪ 2003

This quilt was made with yellow chintz and decorator fabrics I had owned for at least twenty-five years. It's a formal quilt made in the fashion of colonial America when medallion-style quilts were king. Designed and made by Gwen Marston; machine quilted by Robyn House.

Parts *Bias (Serpentine) Strips* (page 84)
Flying Geese (page 90)

Flower Pot on Purple

41" × 45" (104.1 cm × 114.3 cm) ▪ 2006

Over the years, I have returned with regularity to this favorite theme of baskets filled with flowers. Making use of a smashing large-scale print for the flower pot adds drama to this piece. Designed and made by Gwen Marston; machine quilted by Robyn House.

Parts *Diamond Border* (page 88)

Flower Pot on Yellow

53" × 53" (134.6 cm × 134.6 cm) ▪ 2006

Although I worked with traditional methods for designing and cutting the shapes, I gave this quilt a contemporary feeling with my fabric choices. The corners, with their circles framed on two sides in blue, is a design idea I got from a medallion quilt made by "the" Martha Washington. Designed and made by Gwen Marston; machine quilted by Robyn House.

Parts   *Flying Geese* (page 90)

Joseph's Coat Strippy

52" × 61"
(132.1 cm × 154.9 cm)
2004

There is no doubt about it: A quiltmaker can learn plenty by even a casual study of early Amish quilts. Those inventive quilters joined rich color with simple design to create some of the most outstanding quilts made in America. (They had a way with borders, too.) The saturated colors in this quilt were favorites with the Lancaster County Amish prior to World War II. Designed and made by Gwen Marston; machine quilted by Jamie Schantz.

Parts

Spike (page 122)
Strata (page 125)

Liberated Log Cabin in Batiks
A Two-Sided Quilt

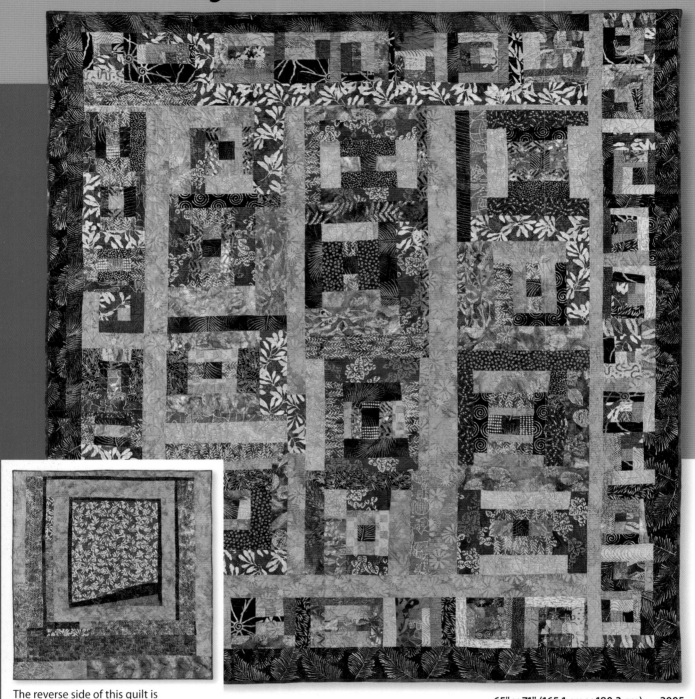

65" × 71" (165.1 cm × 180.3 cm) ▪ 2005

The reverse side of this quilt is constructed as one large Liberated Log Cabin block. Working on this scale looks easy, but for a person who is most comfortable working with a 6" block, this was both exhilarating and challenging.

I continued my exploration of the liberated Log Cabin with this quilt made with batiks, working with larger and less-complex blocks than usual. Note that I went back to using smaller blocks on the borders. Designed and made by Gwen Marston; machine quilted by Robyn House.

Parts *Liberated Log Cabin* (page 100)

Liberated Wedding Ring

61" × 73"
(154.9 cm × 185.4 cm)
1999

I *think* this is my own original block design. Then again, I also recall hearing about a new quilter who thought *she'd* invented a new block—which turned out to be the Nine Patch! Compare this quilt to our collaborative *Liberated Wedding Ring* on page 162; similar parts, totally different palette. Just goes to show that you can make even the most "liberated" of designs in whatever colors you choose. Designed, made, and hand quilted by Gwen Marston.

Parts *Liberated Wedding Ring* (page 106)

Log Cabin in Wool

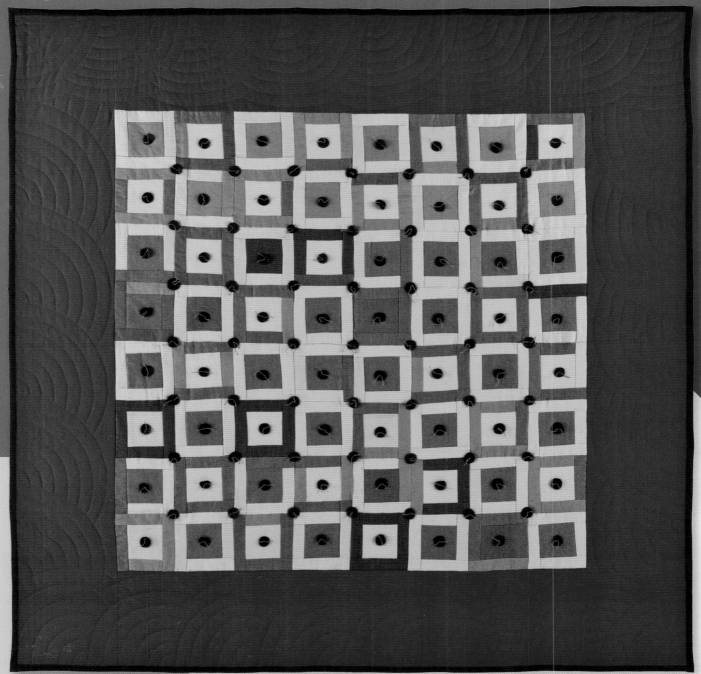

66" × 66" (167.6 cm × 167.6 cm) ▪ 1993

The blocks in this quilt are tied with black felt circles and red floss, an idea inspired by a tied antique quilt. The border is hand quilted in large fans. This is the kind of simple block I like. The square has been around for a long time and I like working with it. Designed, made, tied, and hand quilted by Gwen Marston.

Parts *Log Cabin Variation II* (page 109)

Mason Jar Bouquet

43" × 48" (109.2 cm × 121.9 cm)
2006

I always seem to be working on yet another fabric floral arrangement. This time the flowers are arranged in a Mason jar, a common display in most American homes at one time or another. Designed and made by Gwen Marston; machine quilted by Robyn House.

Parts

Flying Geese (page 90)
Nine Patch (page 112)

Medallion

61" × 57" (154.9 cm × 144.8 cm) ▪ 2002

This is one of a series of medallion quilts I made in 2002. I began by making these quilts in a style I thought Martha Washington would understand—including this one.

The medallion format makes a great showcase for your favorite parts from The Parts Department. Start with something fantastic in the center and build outward from there. Designed, made, and hand quilted by Gwen Marston.

Plum Baskets

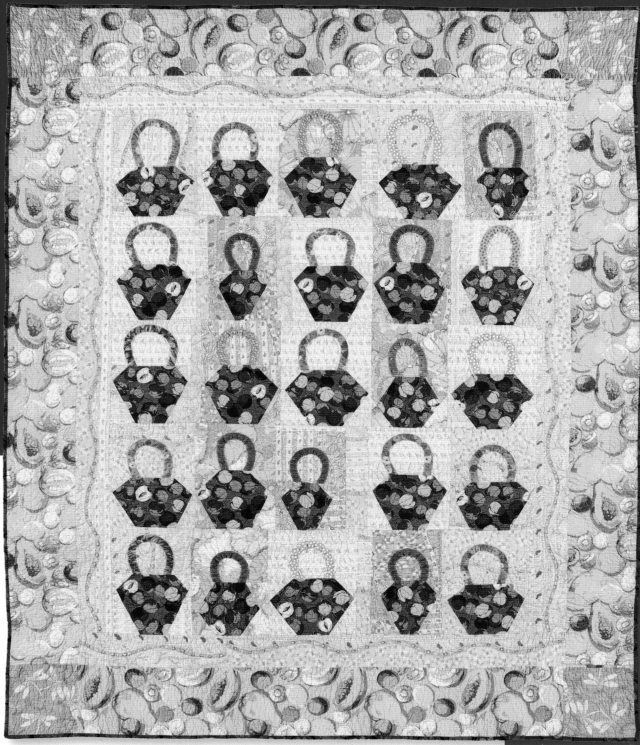

59" × 71"
(149.9 cm × 180.3 cm)
2007

While exploring new shapes for my liberated baskets, I made this playful quilt, using a mix of beautiful contemporary fabrics, for my daughter, Brenda. Designed and made by Gwen Marston; machine quilted by Robyn House.

Parts   *Bias (Serpentine) Strips* (page 84)

Sampler 1

43" × 48" (109.2 cm × 121.9 cm)
2002

This is a scrappy quilt with lots of surprises tucked in. I made and sewed together a variety of odd-sized blocks, using filler strips to make them fit. This construction method was common on samplers made in the 19th century, and by using reproduction fabrics, I was able to re-create further the appearance of those old-fashioned predecessors. (See the antique sampler quilt tops on pages 14 and 15 to compare.) Making a quilt such as this is like working on a jigsaw puzzle—and just as much fun! Designed, made, and hand quilted by Gwen Marston.

Sampler III

56" × 63" (142.2 cm × 160.0 cm) • 2002

I began by piecing a variety of simple, familiar blocks in reproduction prints and then worked out a system for joining them into rows. This seems to have been a common practice for organizing blocks into samplers in the 1900s, and it works just as well now as it did then. Continuing to work in the style of my predecessors, I sewed on the outer Sawtooth borders, letting the strips end as they may, even if that meant lopping off in the middle of a triangle. Designed, made, and hand quilted by Gwen Marston.

Parts

Four Patch (page 92)
Half-Square-Triangle Unit (page 94)
Liberated Star (page 104)
Nine Patch (page 112)
Pinwheel (page 115)

Scrappy Triangle Strippy

42" × 52" (106.7 cm × 132.1 cm)
2003

I used reproduction fabrics reminiscent of the mid-1700s to get the rich look of earlier strippy quilts. The ideas for this quilt came from an antique piece made in Connecticut circa 1840–1865 that I discovered in a book of quilts documented during the Connecticut Quilt Search Project. (See Bibliography, page 189.) Designed, made, and hand quilted by Gwen Marston.

Parts *Half-Square-Triangle Unit* (page 94)

Variable Stars

60" × 70"
(152.4 cm × 177.8 cm)
1991

This quilt was shown at the 1991 American Quilter's Society Show & Contest in Paducah, Kentucky. It was the first Star quilt made in my liberated, free-piecing method. Since then, I have used the liberated methods I developed to make many more Star quilts, and keep busy teaching my methods to other quilters. Designed, made, and hand quilted by Gwen Marston.

Parts

Liberated Log Cabin (page 100)
Liberated Star (page 104)

Whig Rose Medallion

66" × 66" (167.6 cm × 167.6 cm) • 2005

The large center block is my design based on the traditional Whig Rose; the outer border is my design as well. The inside appliqué border was inspired by a circa 1900 quilt made in Wisconsin by Alice Huebner Besau and her daughter, Mary. Designed, made, and hand quilted by Gwen Marston.

Parts *Half-Square-Triangle Unit* (page 94)

Chapter 2

Designing With Freddy: Color... and More

$\mathcal{A}$ lot has changed, and a lot has stayed the same since *Collaborative Quilting* was published in 2006. Just when I thought I had reached the nirvana of quilts and quiltmaking, a new world opened up to me. So many new quilts to make, so little time!

■ Sources of Inspiration? Let Me Count the Ways

The inspiration for a new quilt comes from many sources. The most frequent source for me is Gwen. We are always in contact with each other, so ideas flow back and forth freely.

Fabric is a constant source of inspiration—the color, the scale of the print. Is the print a bold stripe, a large-scale cabbage rose, or a teensy check or rosebud? Happily (for me) there seem to be more large-scale prints available in the quilt stores now, and I love the challenge these fabrics present.

Sometimes I am attracted to a piece of fabric that—no matter how I try—just "doesn't work." I am stubborn enough to keep working with that fabric so sometimes I can pull it off, but most times I know before I am very far into the design that it isn't meant to be. Either way, I've learned an important lesson.

Inspiration can come from a single color—a red quilt perhaps—or from something I discover while looking through magazines or visiting a museum or art gallery. I don't limit myself to quilt books and shows, but expose myself to "experiences" of all kinds, exploring sculpture, collage, painting, and so on.

Inspiration often comes from the classes that I teach. I learn something every time I step into the classroom. Perhaps it is some little thing I see, or something that a student says, and I am off on a new tangent. It might be a new color combination—lime green and French blue or red and periwinkle—or a block enlarged for an entirely new look. As the students work, I might isolate an area of the project I am teaching and decide it would be a good idea to enlarge or repeat it, or to use it in combination with another block.

Teaching challenges me to verbalize my ideas—not only the construction techniques I use, but thoughts about the balance of color, value, and scale in a quilt, or how the eye perceives a composition to identify what it needs to evolve into a homogenous, exciting piece of art.

I approach every class with the goal that the student will add his or her own artistic imprint to the class project, even if it is a "formulaic" quilt. There is always ample opportunity for personal interpretation in a quilt. It might be in the choice of color or fabric, or perhaps the use of value. I encourage each student to make his or her own quilt—not the class sample—and I am exhilarated when this happens.

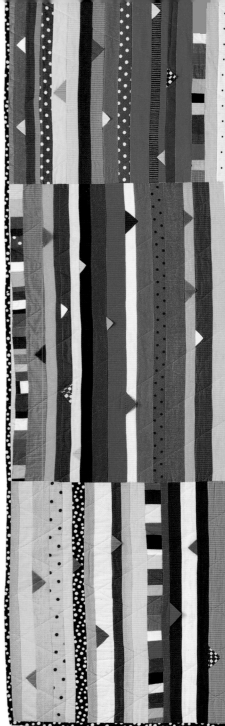

A detail of **Collage House**: Making this quilt was a new experience for me. I constructed the entire top without sewing a stitch. For a full view, see page 51.

I am inspired by new techniques in quiltmaking and especially by collage. I'm proud to say I've glued an entire quilt! I pieced a central design, glued it to a foundation, and built a landscape around it. That quilt, called *Collage House*, appears on page 51 (detail above). I've glued purchased, sequined Madonna images to a pieced background, and embellished the surface with ribbon, trims, shisha mirrors, and other doodads.

If I don't try working with outlandish ideas, I am not progressing in my design capabilities. I need these challenges to keep my work from getting static. I need to challenge myself constantly to grow as an artist.

■ Shoveling Smoke

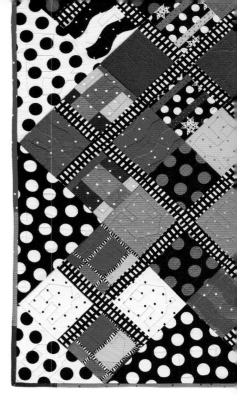

Color is intuitive for me. I consider it an emotional response, and trying to describe it is like "shoveling smoke." Color is a very personal experience. How you approach and use it is based on so many memories and experiences.

I am still experimenting with color in my quilts. I try to use as much color in as many ways as I can without creating total chaos. I rely on black and white to prevent this from happening. The eye can only absorb so much color and then it cries "enough!" It searches for the highest contrast—the black and white—and rests until it says, "Now I can look at more color."

A few years ago I attended a quilt show and saw a perfectly made red and white Pineapple quilt that had been awarded a Judge's Choice ribbon. I looked quickly at the quilt, saw it all in a matter of seconds, and moved on to what I considered the more interesting quilts. I later returned to that red and white quilt and discovered the Judge's Choice ribbon was for Best Use of Color. Now I love red and white as much or more than most, but a two-color quilt with a color award?

I live with lots of color and I always have. I was fortunate early in my quilting career to discover my style, and it really has to do with my use of color. I am very brave in its use, so I will try anything. Why not? All that can happen is that it doesn't work, so I simply take it out and try something else. If I don't try, I'll never progress, and all my quilts will look the same.

■ The Lure — and Power — of Fabric

I usually start a quilt because of a particular fabric. I proceed to select fabrics to complement that particular fabric and each other, and it is only then that I decide how the fabrics will be put together. Sometimes I make some traditional blocks to add to a group of fabrics I've sewn together, and use that as a starting point. I put the pieces on my design wall and move parts and hunks of color around until I have a pleasing and somewhat balanced composition. Trial and error is a big part of my quiltmaking process.

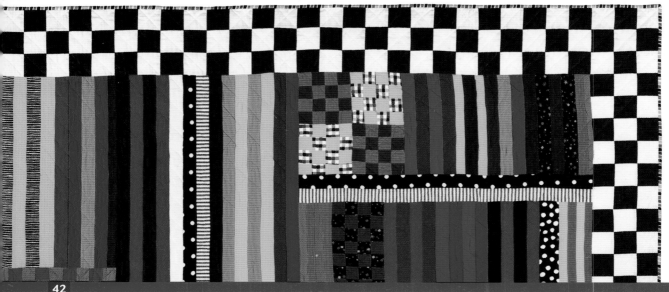

It wasn't always this way for me. Many, many years ago I rejected the idea of quilting, as the only fabrics I saw in quilt shops were calicos in drab colors with very small-scale prints. When I finally reconsidered, the fabrics had changed tremendously. They were brighter, with more variation in print scale. I felt drawn to the colors enough to feel encouraged to try my hand at making a quilt.

Originally, I was drawn—believe it or not—to 1930s-style fabrics, as these prints seemed to be the most colorful. Although small in scale, they were done in what I considered to be bright pastels, and they seemed somewhat larger in scale than typical calicos. I took my first quilting class and made a bright pastel sampler using many '30s-style fabrics. I continued in this color vein for about a year, and then I discovered the book *Quilts! Quilts!! Quilts!!!*. (See Bibliography, page 189.) Although I was still doing everything by hand, I started venturing toward a brighter palette. Red, orange, lime green, purple, and black and white became my new favorites. I made most of the quilts in *Quilts! Quilts!! Quilts!!!*, working alone and by hand.

Eventually, I found the courage to take a class. By now my palette was like nothing I saw around me. I couldn't tell if my quilts were wonderful or hideous. I had no models, as all the quilts I saw in magazines and books were in very subdued colors: lots of grayed blues, greens, beiges, and browns. There seemed to be no brights—just pale pastels: baby blue, baby pink, mint green, egg-yolk yellow, and lots and lots of muslin. The class project was a red and muslin School-house quilt. I made two blocks and I was through. Why would I want to make a dozen blocks that all looked the same? I got out my "stash" and—using the same pattern—switched to my bright colors to make a House quilt that looked like Joseph's Coat of Many Colors.

■ A Quilt Artist is Born

That quilt was the real beginning for me, when I said to myself, "I love this quilt and I no longer care if others find it loud, garish, or jarring." I knew I had found my style and was on my way.

So here I am, hundreds of quilts later, and I am still using my own color palette. Has it changed? A bit. I look at my early post-Schoolhouse quilts and I can see subtle differences. While those early colorful quilts still look great, I believe it is the availability of larger-scale prints in more varied color combinations, coupled with my ability to use various textiles, such as silk, velvet, and rayons, that has led to my newer, "freer" quilts. I know I now have much more confidence as an artist and as a quiltmaker; I am fearless in my color choices and combinations and have developed my own unique style.

■ A Day in the Life…

So, how do I design a quilt today? I recently took a class from quilt artist Elizabeth Barton. The description of the class forecast emphasis on design exercises to develop and strengthen overall composition skills, with the end result a successful

art quilt. I came to the class determined to make just that: a successful art quilt. I looked carefully through my existing Parts Department and came up with the idea of building a village using parts already made and waiting there.

My first decision was background fabric, which would become the sky in my design. Then I began placing bits and pieces and chunks of fabric on my background, starting in the lower left corner and working top to bottom. I worked on my design wall, auditioning various building parts—windows, roofs, doors—adding an occasional tree, a chimney, and more buildings on the lower level, moving colors, and—of course—scattering black and white buildings about.

As I worked in class, a very definite composition began to take shape … but mainly in my mind. I tend to work slowly and poorly in class. I frequently am frustrated by the absence of the right fabric; I know I have the perfect piece I need at home. I need time to be alone with my thoughts, yet I need to be "present" to listen to the instructor. I did some of the exercises and rejected others. I replaced the buildings and left the class with just one-eighth of my composition in place, but with a good feeling about the project overall. I came home, put the work-in-progress on my design wall, and then did nothing to it for about a week.

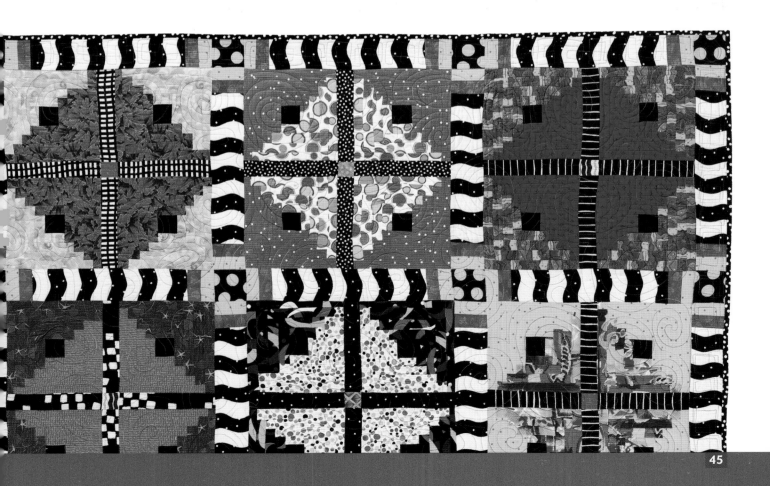

Meanwhile, all of the instructor's lectures and ideas were running around in my brain. I had absorbed a ton of information without realizing it. After about ten days of living with and looking at the quilt, I was able to work very confidently to finish piecing it. I was pleased with the finished quilt when I got it back from the quilter, but the thing I am *most* proud of is that I was able to take a class from a wonderful quilt artist, and yet *I made my own quilt*. It is definitely a "Freddy quilt," not a quilt designed by the instructor.

This has always been a stumbling block for me. How can I take a class from a great teacher/artist and still have my work emerge looking like my own? I have discovered that if I stick to my own color credo and design, by making lots and lots of quilts, I make the important concepts mine. I have my own unique style, and I am staying with it.

Keeping Fresh

I try to take at least one quilt class a year. I am most selective about the teacher, and rarely produce in the classroom, but what I take home in my brain is astounding. I can take what I like and leave the rest. I can work in my own way to achieve my results. I don't take the class to make a copy of the teacher's work. I take the class to try ideas and techniques to help me make my own work.

Taking classes also helps me as a teacher. It reminds me how hard it is to make a public mistake, not understand what is being said, to have my efforts look clumsy and disproportioned. My ego hurts! I must continually remind myself that "this is all about a process," to consider the time spent in class as a learning experience, and to recognize that through practice, the work will improve. In the end, I consider my quilt a success if it looks like my work, and not a poor imitation of the teacher's.

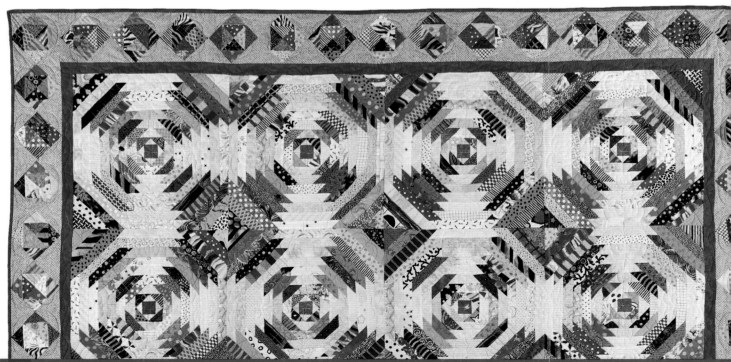

■ Continuing to Grow

Has my use of color changed in order to make quilts using the new techniques I'm trying? I don't think "changing" is the word. I think "evolving" or "expanding" says it better. I am very excited by the large-scale prints now on the market, and this has pushed me to make more quilts in the style of the Gee's Bend quilters; that is, to use big, bold prints and larger pieces of fabric in my designs. The results are always a surprise. When I start a quilt, I never know what the end result will look like, what the predominant color will be, or how large the finished piece will be. These surprises are a great source of adrenaline. I keep moving forward, always adding and subtracting, until a design—or at least a sense of where I am headed— emerges. I might start with one idea only to find a totally different design emerge. When that happens, I've learned just to go with it.

Address Unknown II

32" × 42" (81.2 cm × 106.7 cm)
2002

I needed another House quilt for a class sample and I was immediately drawn to this design. The stars are startling and dramatic, and the black background is the perfect setting for the houses. I love *all* House quilts—especially those done in bright colors. Designed and pieced by Freddy Moran.

Parts   *Liberated Star* (page 104)

American African

54" × 51" (137.2 cm × 129.5 cm) ▪ 2007

I pieced this quilt based on a photo I had seen of an African-American quilt made with brightly colored solids. I find myself drawn to solids more and more. When I sent the top to my quilter, I suggested incorporating patriotic words and stars for the quilting. Designed and pieced by Freddy Moran.

Parts   *Strata* (page 125)

Asilomar Houses

51" × 64"
(129.5 cm × 162.5 cm)
2000

I made this House quilt in a class I took from Karen Stone at the Empty Spools Seminar at Asilomar in coastal California. The class focused on using the paper-piecing method of assembly. I arrived with my houses already made, and designed the various paper-pieced "spiky" sashing and borders. I found it an excellent way to combine blocks of different sizes because I could control the size of the sashing strips. Designed and pieced by Freddy Moran.

Collage House

74" × 68" (188.0 cm × 172.7 cm) ▪ 2003

This quilt was inspired by a book of collage quilts made by Edrica Huws. (See Bibliography, page 189.) I pieced the house, and glued it (yes, glued it) to the bed sheet I used for a base. I then started "landscaping" by adding trees, sky, and a garden, which I also glued into place, cutting and re-cutting as I deemed necessary. What a fun way to build a quilt. You don't even need a sewing machine or a needle. Designed and made by Freddy Moran.

Color Graphics

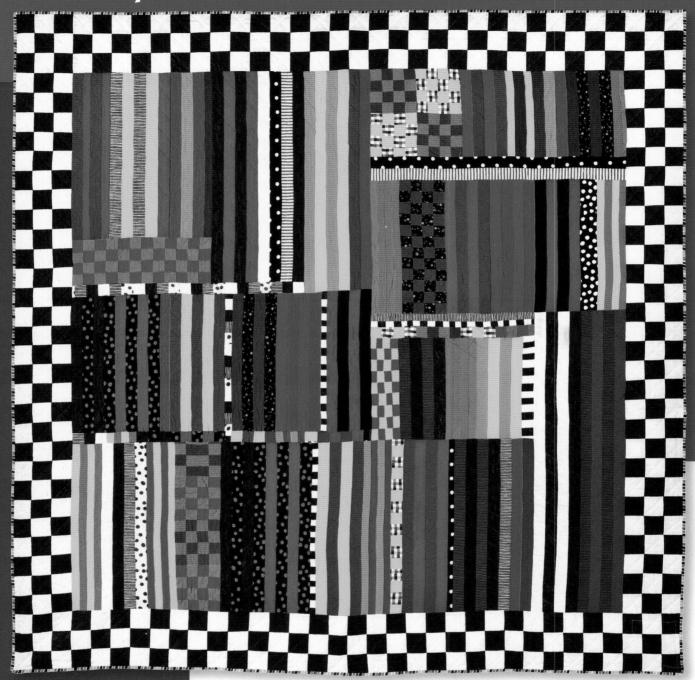

82" × 86" (208.2 cm × 218.4 cm) ▪ 1993

What fun it was to make this quilt. I cut tons of solid-colored strips, put them in a basket, and then pulled them out and pieced them together randomly. When I felt the design needed interruption, I added checks, dots, or stripes to the solids, again relying largely on black and white. As it was difficult to find many black and white geometrics in the early 1990s, I machine pieced the black and white checkerboard border myself. Designed and pieced by Freddy Moran.

Parts *Nine Patch* (page 112)
Strata (page 125)

Fixer Uppers

62" × 67" (157.5 cm × 170.2 cm) ▪ 2000

I recently had remodeled our new home, so the "raw materials-and-unfinished" look was very vivid in my mind. Frequently when I begin a House quilt design, I try to color my houses so they stick out in the neighborhood. Designed and pieced by Freddy Moran.

Parts   *Liberated House* (page 98)

Green Beans

44" × 44" (111.8 cm × 111.8 cm) ▪ 2002

This is my study in green. I used Leaf blocks in three sizes and created a rule that I couldn't use any black and white. Every now and then, I try to wean myself from my "crutch" of black and white. I think I did really well with this quilt; notice that I used this combo only in the leaf stems. Designed and pieced by Freddy Moran.

Parts *Half-Square-Triangle Unit* (page 94)

Liberated Log Cabin X

60" × 65" (152.4 cm × 165.1 cm)
2007

If I could make only one style of quilt from now on, it would be the Log Cabin. The pattern allows such freedom in design, size, and color; there is no definitive right or wrong way to make it. For the block centers here I used scraps given to me by an artist friend. The scraps are from Pakistani Ralli or Snake quilts that are hand quilted in small villages. Be sure to check out *Ralli Double Serpentine* (page 176), our collaborative quilt featuring this unique textile. Designed and pieced by Freddy Moran.

Parts *Liberated Log Cabin* (page 100)
Log Cabin Variation II (page 109)

Magic Squares

54" × 54" (137.2 cm × 137.2 cm) ▪ 2006

This quilt was made in a class I took from Sylvia Einstein. I love putting so many colors and print scales together. The center of the quilt is constructed of squares filled with circles in the same exciting mixture of scale and color. The border is crucial, adding calm and just a bit of color. What an exciting quilt! Designed and pieced by Freddy Moran.

Parts *Sticks* (page 124)

Martin Moran's Quilt

78" × 86" (198.1 cm × 218.4 cm)
1993

I frequently design the "next" quilt while I am working on the present one. Such was the case for this quilt, which followed not long after *Color Graphics* (page 52). I had lots of scraps left over from the previous quilt, so this quilt came to be. My son, Martin, told me he preferred quilts without borders, but when I finished the quilt, I thought it looked naked, so I added the prairie points. Designed and pieced by Freddy Moran.

Parts   *Strata* (page 125)

Four Square Polka Dots

40" × 50"
(101.6 cm × 127.0 cm)
2000

Parts   *Four Patch*
(page 92)

A number of years ago, I designed a line of fabric called Pure Color, geometric prints in bold colors and lots of black and white. I made this baby-size quilt to showcase the fabrics. I am almost all out of the fabric, so I have become very discerning about where and how I use it. Designed and pieced by Freddy Moran.

Oklahoma Chickens

76" × 81" (193.0 cm × 205.7 cm)
2007

While visiting friends in Oklahoma, I saw a bird I couldn't identify. Since I love chickens, all birds seem to become chickens for me—even if they aren't. Once again I mixed color and print scale for the background, and topstitched the birds in place. My quilter added the fried eggs. Designed and pieced by Freddy Moran.

Parts

Diagonal String Block (page 86)
Liberated Log Cabin (page 100)
Strata (page 125)

Pineapple Quilt

80" × 80" (203.2 cm × 203.2 cm) ▪ 1999

This quilt falls within the Log Cabin family and is my idea of the ultimate scrap quilt. It represents a departure for me from my usual palette as it features a neutral, off-white background and no eye-popping black and white. I made this quilt entirely from my scrap bins. I placed the off-white fabrics first, and then used the "pull-from-the-scrap bin" technique to place the colors randomly. I have made about a dozen Pineapple quilts. They are labor intensive to cut and piece, but well worth the effort. Designed and pieced by Freddy Moran.

Pyramids 1

57" × 67"
(144.8 cm × 170.2 cm)
2003

I love, love, *love* these bright pastel prints. I was away from my studio, teaching during the day and working on this quilt in the evenings. I wanted to work with a simple shape that would spotlight the fabrics and be a "no brainer" to construct. I'll admit, I am most happy with the results. Designed and pieced by Freddy Moran.

Parts *Pyramid* (page 118)

Silk Pyramid

54" × 68"
(137.2 cm × 172.7 cm)
2006

Parts *Pyramid*
(page 118)

This is one of a few silk quilts I have made. The colors of the silks are glorious! I was a bit hesitant to tackle silk, but once I realized that I could stabilize it with an iron-on stabilizer, I found it quite easy to work with. The experience was valuable to my learning curve as I am now able to tackle many, many non-traditional textiles in my quilts. Designed and pieced by Freddy Moran.

Split Logs

58" × 78"
(147.3 cm × 198.1 cm)
2001

This vibrant quilt was inspired by the quilts in a book about Log Cabin quilts. The quilt was a joy to create; each block was like starting a whole new quilt project. The presence of black and white is a classic example of how I use these two colors in my quilts. They really make the other colors pop. Designed and pieced by Freddy Moran.

The Orinda Hills

50" × 50" (127.0 cm × 127.0 cm) ▪ 1999

Shortly after we moved to our "house on the hill," I found myself inspired by the houses I passed on my way home. I love the reds in this piece. I striped lots and *lots* of red fabrics for the background—red is a neutral, you know. Designed and pieced by Freddy Moran.

Parts *Liberated House* (page 98)
Liberated Log Cabin (page 100)
Strata (page 125)

Wedding Ring

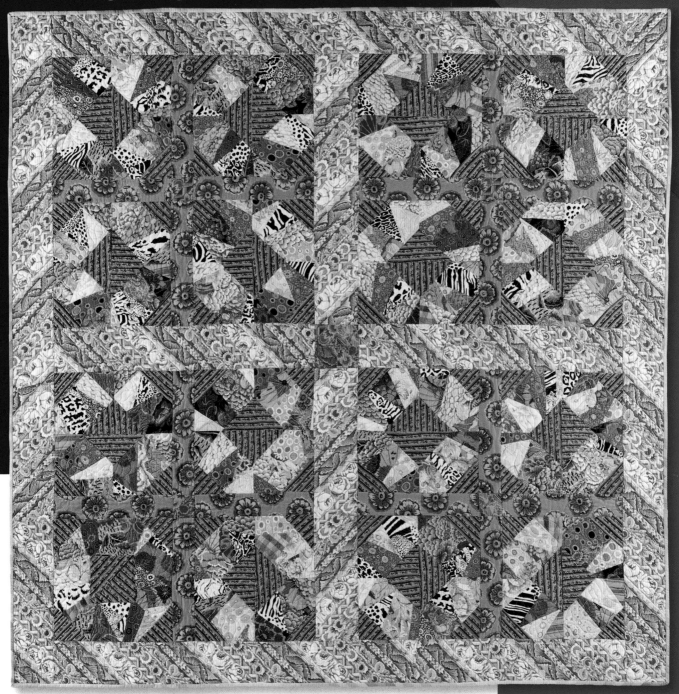

73" × 73" (185.4 cm × 185.4 cm) ▪ 2006

I made this bright pastel quilt after a quilting session with Gwen. This is her version of a Wedding Ring, and it is based on an antique quilt format of four repeating blocks. Look at what the black and white does for this quilt; it keeps the eye moving around and around. Designed and pieced by Freddy Moran.

Parts *Liberated Wedding Ring* (page 106)

Windows

62" × 62" (157.5 cm × 157.5 cm) ▪ 1995

I am amazed when I look at this quilt 13 years after making it. I realize I was making Parts Department quilts all those years ago. The black background really "pops" the color and I like the shiny thread in the quilting. Designed and pieced by Freddy Moran.

Parts *Log Cabin Variation I* (page 108)
Sticks (page 124)

You're a Life Saver

80" × 80" (203.2 cm × 203.2 cm) ▪ 1999

Essentially, this is a color study that uses mainly batiks. It is the first of what I call my "circle quilts" and is quieter and less textured than most of my work. I tried many fabrics for the border, but found that black and white worked best. This quilt was accepted into the Quilt San Diego Visions exhibit in 1998. Designed and pieced by Freddy Moran.

Chapter 3

Nuts and Bolts: Tools and Techniques for Making These Quilts

Every quilter has a list of tools he or she considers essential for making quilts, and preferences for certain techniques to get the job done. We're no different, and that's what this chapter is all about. Even if you have been quilting for a long time, you might want to take a peek.

The Basic Tool Kit

As you turn the page, you'll find the things we couldn't do without as we went about creating our collaborative quilts. We refer to this Basic Tool Kit often in the chapter on our collaborative work.

Needles and Pins

There are lots of them out there, and the best way to find out what works for you is to experiment. As far as needles go, our one non-negotiable is that the eye is large enough to accept the thread easily. This can vary greatly from brand to brand, so it pays to shop around.

When it comes to pins, we like those nice, sturdy quilter's pins. They are terrific for fastening parts and works-in-progress to your design surface, and you also can use them for most tasks involved with quilt assembly. However, you'll also want to have a supply of thin, fine pins (called silk pins) in your sewing room to use for performing more refined work or for those times when you are working with more delicate fabrics.

Thread

Cotton thread is our thread of choice for piecing our quilts. It's sturdy, readily available, comes in lots of colors, and is a good match for cotton fabrics. It is also what many sewing machine manufacturers recommend.

Rotary Cutter, Rulers, and Cutting Mat

When viewing some of the wonderful pieced quilts of the 19th and early 20th centuries—Log Cabins or Postage Stamps, for example—it's hard to imagine that all those strips and pieces were cut without the aid of a rotary cutter. We think that just about any quilter today would agree that—next to the sewing machine—it is the most timesaving and indispensable tool available to us. Make sure to keep your cutter outfitted with a sharp blade, and keep extras handy so you can replace a blade as soon as it begins to dull … even if it's 3 a.m.

To go with your cutter, you'll want a versatile collection of sturdy, accurate, and well-marked acrylic rulers. We've found the most helpful sizes are 6" × 6" (15.2 cm × 15.2 cm), 6" × 12" (15.2 cm × 30.5 cm), 6" × 24" (15.2 cm × 61.0 cm), and 12" × 12" (30.5 cm × 30.5 cm). We use them constantly to cut strips and pieces, to square blocks to size, and to trim and square the edges of our quilts.

Finally, you'll want a firm, flat, safe surface to cut on. A self-healing cutting mat does the trick. Again, these come in various sizes and with grids to mark off inches and angles. Your personal requirements and your workspace will determine which works best for you.

Scissors

No matter how versatile, the rotary cutter still has not managed to replace the scissors in the quilter's tool kit. There are times when nothing else will do. We keep a small, sharp pair of scissors or snips nearby for clipping threads and for general "housekeeping."

■Quilt Class: Helpful Techniques

This section won't tell you *everything* you need to know about making a quilt, but it will give you helpful information specific to making the parts and adding the touches to make them into quilts.

Cutting Half- and Quarter-Square Triangles

Many parts in The Parts Department (page 76) call for half-square and quarter-square triangles. The difference between cutting a half- or a quarter-square triangle is all about where you want the non-stretchy straight grain to fall: on the short, right angle edges or on the long, diagonal edge. Whenever possible, it's nice to have the straight grain fall on the outside edge of the part, block, or quilt. There will always be exceptions—and it is almost impossible to worry about straight grain with some of the liberated parts—but when you are working with right angle triangles, you always have this option.

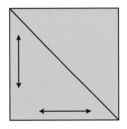

Fig. 1

    If you want the straight grain to fall on the short, right angle edge of the triangle, cut a square, and then cut the square in half from corner to corner in *one* direction: a half-square triangle (fig. 1).

    If you want the straight grain to fall on the long diagonal edge of the triangle, cut a square, and then cut the square in half from corner to corner in *both* directions: a quarter-square triangle (fig. 2).

    There is an easy way to figure how large to cut the squares in order to have adequate seam allowance for the resulting triangles.

    For **half-square triangles**, determine the *finished measurement* you need, and then add ⅞" (2.2 cm). For example, for a 4" (10.2 cm) finished measurement, you'll need to cut the square 4⅞" (12.4 cm).

    For **quarter-square triangles**, determine the *finished measurement* you need, and then add 1¼" (3.2 cm). For a 4" (10.2 cm) finished unit, you'll need to cut the square 5¼" (13.3 cm).

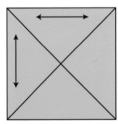

Fig. 2

    Pretty handy stuff! *So* handy that you just might want to mark this page. You'll come back to it over and over, not just for parts, but also for figuring out how to cut triangles for setting blocks on point and so forth.

Setting Blocks on Point

A number of our collaborative quilts—for example, *Beautiful Baskets* (page 142) and *Definitely Gee's Bend* (page 148)—have sashing or borders with blocks set on point. To accomplish this, you'll need to cut triangles to "set things straight." Make sure to cut these setting triangles so their long, diagonal edge is on the straight grain. This means you'll be cutting quarter-square triangles.

1. First figure the size of the squares you'll need. (Hint: It will be the finished size of the block you are setting set on point + 1¼" [**3.2 cm**].) Cut the necessary number of squares (remember: each square yields four triangles), and then cut the squares diagonally in both directions.

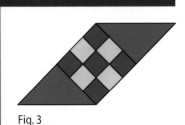

Fig. 3

2. Sew two triangles to each block (fig. 3).

3. Sew the units together and press.

Adding Sashing

A number of our quilts use sashing; that is, strips sewn between the blocks to frame and separate them. Sometimes there are two layers of sashing: One layer separates groups of blocks into fours, reminiscent of antique four-block quilts, and then a second layer separates these four-block sections. Depending upon the fabrics you use, you can create wonderful dimensional effects. Sometimes—if you're lucky—this occurs as a happy accident.

Sashing strips can be cut to the same width throughout, or they can vary as you wish. You can run sashing vertically, horizontally, or in both directions. It can be pieced or plain. Even diagonally set quilts can have sashing. There are precedents for all in antique quilts.

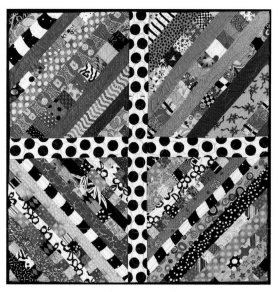

Detail of *1937 Revisited*: An example of a simple sashing treatment.

To set four blocks with sashing:

1. Arrange the blocks and sashing strips as shown. Sew a short vertical sashing strip between two blocks (fig. 4). Press toward the sashing strip. Make two.

2. Sew the long horizontal strip between the two rows (fig. 5). Press toward the sashing strip.

Fig. 4

Fig. 5

Detail of *Beautiful Baskets*: The diminutive (2" [5.1 cm] finished) Four Patches in this pieced sashing balance nicely with the larger-scale Basket blocks.

Sewing on Borders

You've probably noticed that some of the quilts in this book—both our individual quilts and our collaborative work—do not have borders. This is nothing new. Many 19th and early 20th-century quilts did not have borders, or only had borders on one, two, or three sides. It worked then, and it still works today.

For our quilts that *do* include borders, we often relied on a simple, straightforward approach: We used butt joints at the corners. We typically added the side borders first, and then sewed on the top and borders.

1. Press the quilt top so it lies as flat as possible. Spread it on the floor or another flat surface.

2. Measure the quilt down the center from top to bottom and cut two borders to that measurement. Mark the midpoints of the sides of the quilt and the border strips (fig. 6). Place a border along the edge of the quilt.

3. Pin the ends of the quilt and the border right sides together. Pin the border to the quilt at the marked midpoints. Keep dividing the pinned sections into smaller sections until the border is uniformly and flatly pinned to the quilt.

4. Sew and press. Repeat to pin and sew the other side border.

5. Measure the quilt across the center from side to side, including the borders you just added. Cut two borders to that measurement. Mark the midpoints on the top and bottom of the quilt and on the border strips (fig. 7).

6. Pin, sew, and press.

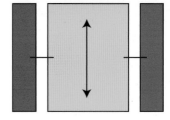

Fig. 6

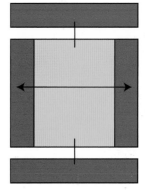

Fig. 7

Pressing Bias for Sashing and Borders

Pressing bias strips into shape eliminates puckers on the inside curves and makes the whole job of sewing bias to sashing and borders much easier.

1. Cut the sashing or borders for your quilt. Make them an inch or two longer than necessary. You will cut them to length once the bias is sewn in place.

2. Lay the border on the ironing board. Use your right hand to *very gently* pull and position the bias, while your left hand guides the iron in hot pursuit. A spritz of water or starch will stabilize the curving bias like nobody's business.

3. Keep the border with the pressed bias right there on the ironing board. Don't move it! Carefully slip a long (e.g., 6" × 24" [15.2 cm × 61.0 cm]) quilter's ruler under the border and pin the bias in place before it can shift. Silk pins work best because they are long and fine. Pin every 2" (5.1 cm) to 3" (7.6 cm), placing the pins perpendicular to the bias.

Sewing Bias by Machine

Note: You can use matching thread or contrasting thread in your machine.

1. Set the machine to take a small stitch. Experiment and see what you like.

2. Stitch along one side of the bias, staying right on the edge and taking pins out as you come to them.

3. When you get to the end, sew across to the other side and stitch it in place. There is no need to re-pin. Nothing will shift.

4. When you are finished, press the finished border and congratulate yourself on a job well done.

Tying

Forget whatever you may have heard; tying is a great alternative to quilting, especially for scrappy, string-pieced, and large-scale Strata-based designs. This was a common practice in the old days, particularly for utility quilts. We used it for three of the collaborative quilts in this book and we love the way it looks. The ties add texture and color to introduce a whole new element of design.

You'll need a needle with an eye capable of accepting the fiber you use and sturdy enough to pierce the layers to make the ties. We used wool to make the ties in our quilts, but you can also use cotton embroidery floss, pearl cotton, crochet thread, or tatting thread. Stay away from silk—it doesn't stay tied.

While a simple square knot works perfectly, you can embellish your ties as Gwen did in her quilt *Log Cabin in Wool* (page 28).

Finishing the Edges

We've used two different methods for finishing the edges of our quilts: a mitered-corner binding method and a back-to-front finishing method.

The Binding Method

1. Cut the binding 1¼" (3.2 cm) on the straight grain for a single binding, 2¼" (5.7 cm) on the bias for a double-thickness binding. Piece the binding strips together to achieve the necessary length (fig. 8). The total measurement of all four sides plus an extra 10" (25.4 cm) or so for seams, turning the corners, and joining the ends is usually sufficient.

2. Cut the starting end of the binding at a 45-degree angle. This will be important when you join the two ends later.

3. Trim the batting and backing even with the quilt top. For a single binding, align the binding with the edge of the quilt, right sides together. For a double-thickness binding, fold the binding strip in half lengthwise, wrong sides together, and align the raw edges with the edge of the quilt. Begin stitching the binding to the quilt in the middle of one side, leaving 4" (10.2 cm) of the end free.

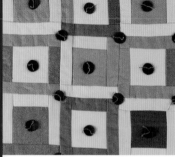

Detail of *Log Cabin in Wool*: Gwen embellished the ties in this quilt by using them to anchor little circles cut from contrasting felt.

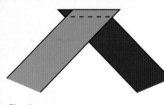

Fig. 8

4. To miter the binding, stop ¼" (0.3 cm) before you reach the first corner. Lift the presser foot and pull the quilt away from the sewing machine.

5. Fold the binding up and away from the quilt at a 45-degree angle (fig. 9).

6. Fold the binding back down so that the raw edges of the binding are aligned with the next edge of the quilt. Return the quilt to the sewing machine, place the needle back into the quilt ¼" (0.3 cm) from both sides of the corner, and resume sewing (fig. 10).

7. Stop sewing when you are about 6" (15.2 cm) away from the place you began stitching the binding to the quilt.

8. Lay the end of the binding over the end you left loose when you started stitching (fig. 11). Draw a pencil line at a 45-degree angle, ½" (1.3 cm) beyond the binding underneath. Trim the top strip ½" (1.3 cm) past the drawn line.

9. Join the two ends, finger press the seams open, and finish stitching the binding to the quilt (fig. 12).

10. Turn the binding to the wrong side of the quilt. For a single binding, roll under a ¼" (0.3 cm) seam allowance and blind stitch the binding in place. For a double binding, simply stitch down the finished edge.

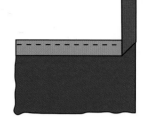

Fig. 9

Fig. 10

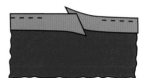

Fig. 11

Fig. 12

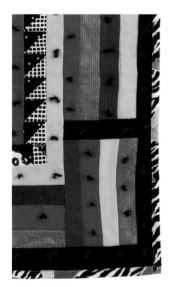

The back-to-front method of finishing a quilt is a common traditional choice. The corners are squared and turned with a small triangle of stitches.

The Back-to-Front Method

In times past, this was a popular way to finish the edges of a quilt. It requires no additional fabric for binding. It struck us as an especially fine way to finish the edges of the tied quilts we made for this book.

1. Using scissors, carefully trim the batting so it is even with the edges of the quilt top.

2. Using a rotary cutter and quilter's ruler, trim the backing to ¾" (1.9 cm) beyond the edge of the quilt top all around.

3. Fold the backing around to the front of the quilt so the raw edge of the backing meets the raw edge of the quilt top. Fold the edge over again to make a finished edge. Fold the corners neatly to square them. Pin about every 2" (5.1 cm).

4. Using matching thread, sew the edge down by hand or machine.

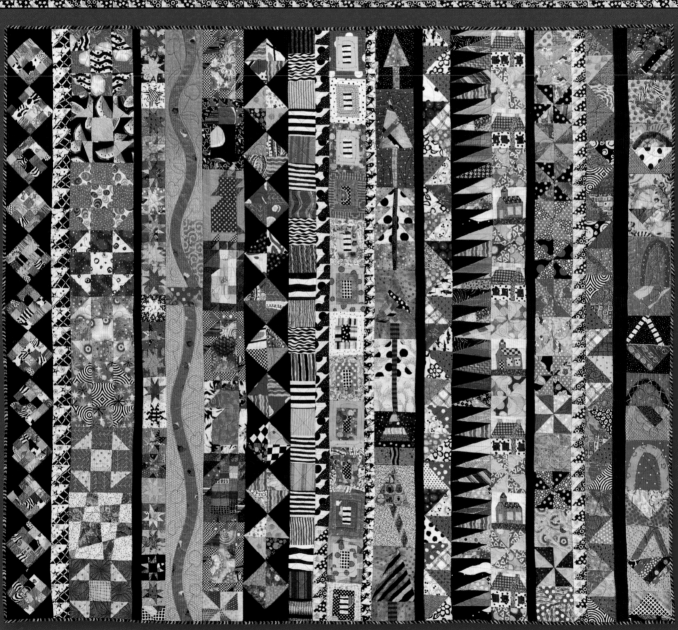

Chapter 4

80" × 66" (203.2 cm × 167.6 cm) ▪ 2006

The Parts Department: Take Two

 ou can use the parts in this chapter to make the quilts in the gallery of this book, or you can do as we did in *Leftovers*: Make a bunch of parts similar in style and then use them to create a unique version of the old-fashioned sampler quilts like the ones shown on pages 14 and 15.

■ Designing with Parts

Leftovers

We thought this quilt would make a good opener for this second edition of The Parts Department. The quilt includes lots of parts from *Collaborative Quilting*, some of which are given a fresh treatment here, in addition to some new ones.

We found that we could make better use of our time together if we made "the parts" on our own and had them ready to use when we got together to work. Since we live across the country from each other, having a well-stocked parts department was an excellent solution and it enabled us to make the 61 quilts shown in our two collaborative books.

Designing with parts takes the mystery out of the design process. With the parts already made, it's easy to explore different layouts because you can actually see what the design will look like. It's just like when you are shopping for a new outfit; you get to try it on, see what it looks like, and see if it fits.

■ Adapting Traditional Formats

We relied on traditional formats long known to quiltmakers that work as well today as they ever did. We simply got out our parts and put them on the design wall in one of the following formats. Often we tried placing them in several different ways and generally that was enough for us to see which way would work best with the blocks we were working with. Also, we didn't think about the borders until we got to them. You don't have to figure out the whole quilt to get started, and we think you will make better choices if you *don't* figure it all out before you start. For example, let's say you are making a medallion quilt. Begin with the center and get that together. The center will help inform you about what might come next. You can make the whole quilt that way, by making decisions just one border at a time.

Medallion Quilts

A medallion quilt is defined as a quilt that has a center area of interest surrounded by a series of borders. The center can be a pieced or appliquéd block, or a whole-cloth panel. Medallion quilts were among the earliest styles of American quilts, coming to the new land with the earlier settlers. Their popularity waned when the block style began to dominate the scene around 1840. Yet medallions continue to be made and we used this format repeatedly and happily when designing many of our quilts. Examples include *It's All About Triangles* (page 158), *Around the Block* (page 138), and *What a Star!* (page 186).

Gwen's **Whig Rose Medallion** is a textbook example of a traditional, medallion-style quilt. For a larger view, see page 36.

… traditional formats long known to quiltmakers … work as well today as they ever did.

Strippy quilts can be made with plain strips, pieced strips, or a combination of the two, as is the case in Gwen's very traditional **Scrappy Triangle Strippy**. For a larger view, see page 34.

Strippy Quilts

Popular in the British Isles as early as 1780, quilts made in long vertical strips were called strippy quilts. Naturally, this style found its way to America as well, but strippy quilts never reached the height of popularity attained by the more elegant medallion style. The good news is, the strippy has made a comeback in recent years with the popularity of the row quilt, made with rows of blocks set either vertically or horizontally.

This format works well when you are building a quilt with your Parts Department, and we've made quite a few strippy quilts, including *Chinese Coins* (page 144), *Spikes* (page 184), and *Posies* (page 172).

Technically, there are two main issues to think about as you work on arranging the rows.

- The blocks must be the same size in one direction only. For example, if you are making a strippy quilt with vertical rows, the blocks only need to be the same *width* so you can sew them into a row.

- Building vertical rows with blocks of different sizes means that the rows will most likely not finish the same length. Your options are to add filler strips or pieces to the shorter rows, or cut off the longer rows. One way or the other, all rows must be the same length. If you want to see our solutions, look at the bottom edges of each of our strippy quilts.

Four-Block Quilts

This is a setting we neglected in *Collaborative Quilting*, so we made up for it in this book with lots of examples—*1937 Revisited* (page 134) and *Beautiful Baskets* (page 142), to name just two.

Four-block quilts are just that: quilts made with four large blocks. In their heyday (between 1850–1880), most four-block quilts were appliqué quilts, though some were pieced. Whether appliquéd or pieced, these quilts tended to be big, strong, bold, splashy quilts. Gwen has made piles of four-block appliqué quilts, so as the designer in this collaborative effort, she was obviously tardy in bringing this format to the table.

Block-to-Block on the Straight or on the Diagonal

This is certainly the most common format in the history of American quilt-making. It clearly depends on working with blocks that are all the same size. We have a number of these quilts in this book—for example, *Damask Log Cabin* (page 146)—but we play fast and loose with the size issue by introducing our liberated style.

Despite its 21st-century appearance, **Wedding Ring**, made by Freddy, is very much in keeping with the 19th-century, four-block tradition. For a larger view, see page 65.

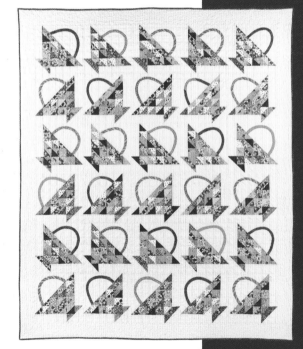

Baskets with Dog Tooth Handles and **Betty and Maude's Baskets**: two "new" quilts, two classic settings. Both quilts by Gwen. For larger views, see pages 18 and 19.

■ Get Ready to Go!

All righty, then. We've talked about design and color, giving you lots of ideas for how to plan your quilts by taking full advantage of lessons from the past and pairing them with the fabrics and techniques of today. Time now to give you the "parts" for creating your own unique 21st-century heirloom. So, turn the page, and let's get started.

Basket with Sawtooth Handle

Appears in

Baskets with Sawtooth Handles (page 140)

Cutting

For one 20"-square (50.8 cm) finished block, cut:

▶ Three 4⅞" (12.4 cm) squares from background fabric, cut into six small half-square triangles. You will use five.

▶ One 4½" (11.4 cm) square from background fabric

▶ Two 4½" × 12½" (11.4 cm × 31.8 cm) rectangles from background fabric

▶ One 8⅞" (22.5 cm) square from background fabric, cut into two medium half-square triangles. You will use one.

▶ One 16⅞" (42.9 cm) square from background fabric, cut into two large half-square triangles. You will use one.

▶ Six 4⅞" (12.4 cm) squares from contrasting (basket) fabric, cut into twelve small half-square triangles. You will use eleven.

Assembly

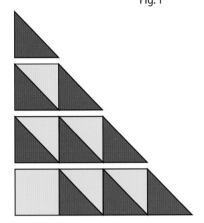

1. Sew small background and basket triangles together (fig. 1). Press. Make five.

2. Arrange and sew triangle units, four small basket triangles, and 4½" (11.4 cm) background square into rows (fig. 2). Press. Sew rows together. Press.

3. Cut and appliqué a handle to large background triangle.

4. Arrange basket unit, appliquéd triangle, two background rectangles, two small basket triangles, and medium background triangle (fig. 3). Sew basket unit and appliquéd triangle together. Press. Sew rectangles and basket triangles together; press and sew to sides of block. Press. Sew medium background triangle to block (fig. 4). Press.

Fig. 1

Fig. 2

Fig. 3

Fig. 4

Taking It from Tradition . . .

Gwen cut the basket handles freehand from folded fabric and therefore they are all a bit different.

Bias (Serpentine) Strips

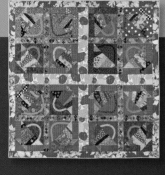

Cutting

▶ Cut strips in desired width from bias of fabric (fig. 1). We cut 1¼"-wide (3.2 cm) strips for *In Your Dreams* and the stems on *Posies*, and 2¼"-wide (5.7 cm) bias strips for *Beautiful Baskets*, *Ralli Double Serpentine*, and the vertical panels of *Posies*.

Fig. 1

Assembly

1. Join bias strips together (fig. 2). Press.

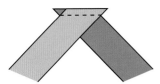

Fig. 2

2. Set sewing machine for basting stitch. Turn raw edges of strip to wrong side, overlapping them slightly. Sew down center (fig. 3).

Fig. 3

3. Position bias in gentle curves on background fabric. Place silk pins perpendicular to strip every 2" (5.1 cm) to 3" (7.6 cm) (fig. 4).

Fig. 4

4. Use small topstitch to sew very close to both edges of curved strip, removing pins as you go (fig. 5). Remove basting and press.

Fig. 5

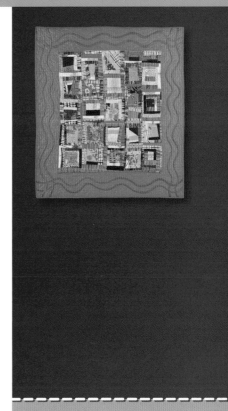

Quilt Class

True bias is cut at a 45-degree angle, but in this case, close is good enough.

When sewing down bias strips, use matching thread if you don't want the stitching to be obvious, contrasting thread if you regard it as a design element.

See Pressing Bias for Sashing and Borders (page 73) and Sewing Bias by Machine (page 74) for more detailed information on pressing, positioning, and sewing bias to your quilt top.

Diagonal String Block

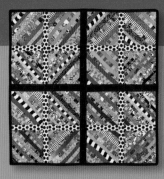

Appears in

1937 Revisited (page 134)
Liberated Red Squares (page 160)

Cutting

▶ Cut assorted strips to the same width for a uniform look. For a liberated effect (and a look more in keeping with antique quilts), cut strips in various widths (e.g., 1¼" [3.2 cm] to 3" [7.6 cm]).

Assembly

1. Sew strips together along their long edges to make a strip set (fig. 1). Essentially, you are "manufacturing" new fabric. Press.

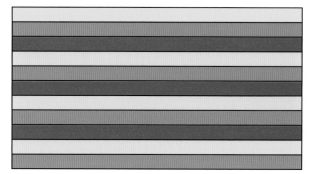

Fig. 1

2. Place a 6" × 24" (15.2 cm × 61.0 cm) ruler on one corner of new "fabric" at a 45-degree angle and cut off corner. Continue moving ruler along strip set at regular intervals to cut diagonal strips of desired width (fig. 2).

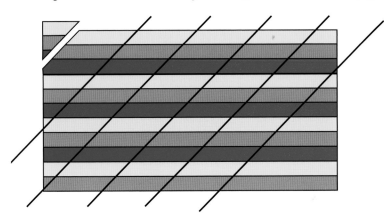

Fig. 2

3. Place each diagonal strip horizontally on cutting board and cut into equal segments (fig. 3).

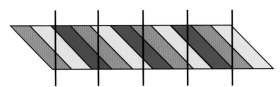

Fig. 3

Diamond Border

Appears in

Liberated Red Squares (page 160)

Cutting

For one 3" × 6" (7.6 cm × 15.2 cm) finished unit, cut:

▶ One 3½" × 6½" (8.9 cm × 16.5 cm) rectangle from one fabric

▶ Two 3½" (8.9 cm) squares from contrasting fabric

Assembly

1. Align one square with one end of rectangle. Sew square from corner to corner (fig. 1).

Fig. 1

2. Trim seam allowance to ¼" (0.3 cm) (fig. 2).

Fig. 2

3. Press unit open (fig. 3).

Fig. 3

4. Align remaining square on opposite end (fig. 4). Sew, trim, and press (fig. 5).

Fig. 4

Fig. 5

5. Sew desired number of units together (fig. 6). Press.

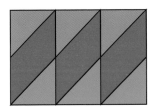

Fig. 6

6. For an alternative version, make half of units as described above, and make other half as shown (fig. 7). Sew desired number of units together, alternating them to create zigzag effect (fig. 8).

Fig. 7

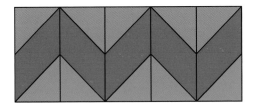

Fig. 8

Flying Geese

Appears in

Definitely Gee's Bend (page 148)
Posies (page 172)

Cutting

For one 2" × 4" (5.1 cm × 10.2 cm) finished part, cut:

▶ One 2½" × 4½" (6.4 cm × 11.4 cm) rectangle from one fabric

▶ Two 2½" (6.4 cm) squares from contrasting fabric

Assembly

1. Align one square with one end of rectangle.
Sew square from corner to corner (fig. 1).

Fig. 1

2. Trim seam allowance to ¼" (0.3 cm) (fig. 2).

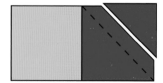

Fig. 2

3. Press unit open (fig. 3).

Fig. 3

4. Align remaining square on opposite end. Sew, trim, and press (fig. 4).

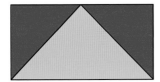

Fig. 4

Taking It from Tradition . . .

Reverse the value placement for a completely different look (fig. 5).

Fig. 5

Four Patch

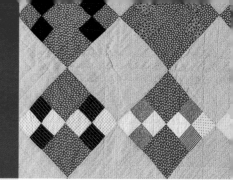

Appears in

Beautiful Baskets (page 142)

Cutting

For multiple 2"-square (5.1 cm) finished parts, cut:

▶ One 1½"-wide (3.8 cm) strip each from two contrasting fabrics

Assembly

1. Sew strips together along their long edges. Press. Cut into 1½"-wide (3.8 cm) segments (fig. 1).

2. Sew two segments together (figs. 2 and 3). Press.

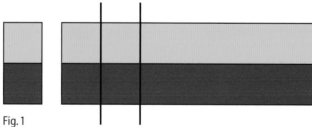

Fig. 1

Fig. 2

Fig. 3

Quilt Class

When making lots of these parts, cut strips in short lengths to guarantee a scrappy outcome. Just so you know: a 40"-long (101.6 cm) strip set yields about twenty-six 1½" (3.8 cm) segments.

Gee's Bend a la California

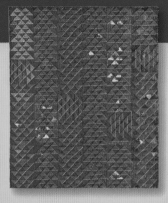

Appears in

Gee's Bend a la California (page 152)

Cutting

For one 3" × 9" (7.6 cm × 22.9 cm) finished part, cut:

▶ Two 3" (7.6 cm) squares from one fabric; cut into four small half-square triangles. You will use three.

▶ One 4" (10.2 cm) square from same fabric; cut into two large half-square triangles.

▶ Three 3" (7.6 cm) squares from contrasting fabric; cut into six small half-square triangles. You will use five.

Assembly

1. Sew one of each small contrasting triangle together (fig. 1). Press. Make two.

Fig. 1

2. Arrange triangle units and remaining small and large triangles (fig. 2). Sew small triangles to triangle units. Press.

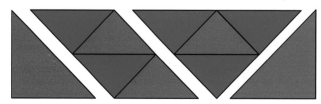

Fig. 2

3. Sew units and large triangles together (fig. 3). Press. Square corner of unit if needed.

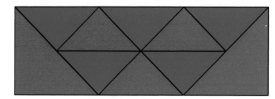

Fig. 3

Half-Square-Triangle Unit

Appears in

Assembly

1. Determine desired finished size of Half-Square-Triangle Unit.

2. Use formula on page 71 to determine cut size of required square. Cut squares from two contrasting fabrics. Each square will make two units.

3. Cut each square in half on the diagonal (fig. 1).

4. Sew contrasting triangles together in pairs along their long diagonal edges (fig. 2). Press.

Fig. 1   Fig. 2

Fig. 3

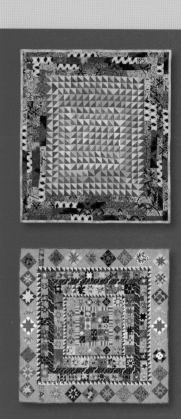

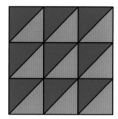

Fig. 4

Fig. 5

Fig. 6

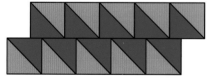

Fig. 7

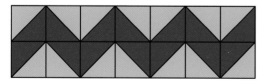

Fig. 8

Fig. 9

Liberated Churn Dash

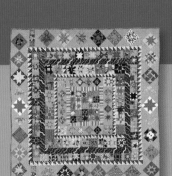

Appears in

What a Star! (page 186)

Cutting

For one 4½"-square (11.4 cm) finished block, cut:

▶ Five 2" (5.1 cm) squares from background fabric

▶ One 1¼" × 8" (3.2 cm × 20.3 cm) strip from background fabric

▶ Two 2½" (6.4 cm) squares from contrasting fabric; cut into four half-square triangles

▶ One 1¼" × 8" (3.2 cm × 20.3 cm) strip from same contrasting fabric

Assembly

1. With right sides together, position triangle on right side of 2" (5.1 cm) background square. Before you sew, fold triangle back to make sure it will cover square completely. Sew triangle to square (fig. 1). Press triangle open from front side. Make four, shifting triangle slightly to vary corner triangle units.

Fig. 1

2. Turn unit over and trim edges of triangle even with square (fig. 2). Turn unit over to front side and press again.

Fig. 2

3. Sew 1¼"-wide (3.2 cm) background and contrasting strips together along their long edges. Press. Place ruler on strip set at slight angle. Cut four 2"-wide (5.1 cm) segments (fig. 3).

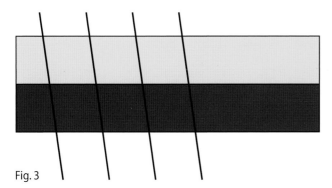

Fig. 3

4. Trim ends so each segment measures 2" (5.1 cm) (fig. 4).

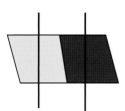

Fig. 4

5. Arrange units, segments, and remaining 2" (5.1 cm) background square and sew them into rows (fig. 5). Press. Sew rows together. Press.

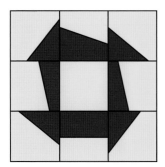

Fig. 5

Liberated House

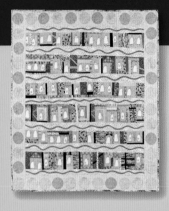

Appears in

In Your Dreams (page 156)

Assembly

1. Cut figure you want to live in your house. Figure can be anything from a rectangle or square to a more abstract shape.

2. Sew strips of assorted fabrics to both sides or one side of shape as desired (fig. 1).

Fig. 1

3. There are two ways to "raise the roof": Place house unit near corner of roof fabric. Cut triangle of roof fabric along edge of unit (fig. 2). Sew triangle to top of house.

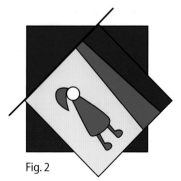

Fig. 2

OR

Sew rectangle of roof fabric to top of house unit (fig. 3). Press. Fold unit in half and make an angled cut (fig. 4).

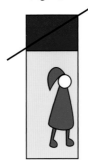

Fig. 3   Fig. 4

4. Fold sky fabric right sides together and position house in corner. Cut sky fabric along edge of roof (fig. 5). This produces both right and left sky triangles.

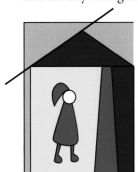

Fig. 5

5. Sew sky triangles to house unit. Press, and then square corners. Add additional strips as desired (fig. 6). Press.

Fig. 6

Liberated Log Cabin

Appears in

Damask Log Cabin (page 146)
In Your Dreams (page 156)
Pinwheels (page 170)
Ralli Double Serpentine (page 176)

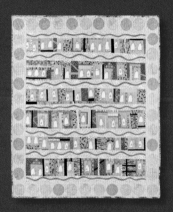

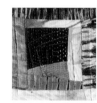

Assembly

1. Freehand cut a center square or rectangle; that is, cut without measuring.

2. Add pieces or strips of varying widths and fabrics in any order around the center shape, trimming them to fit. Press.

3. To create interesting angles, add straight pieces and press. Trim outer edge at an angle (fig. 1). Sew another piece to angled edge. Press and straighten new edge (figs. 2–4).

4. Continue adding strips until block is somewhat larger than desired size.

5. Press block flat from front first, and then flip over and press again, pressing all seams toward outer edges.

6. Trim block to desired size (fig. 5).

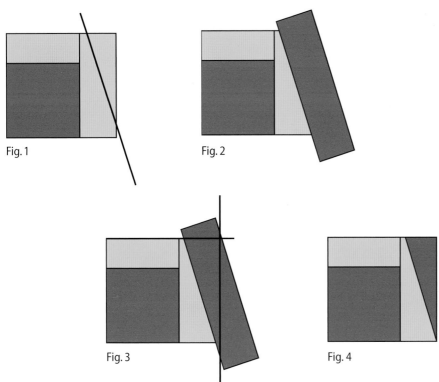

Fig. 1

Fig. 2

Fig. 3

Fig. 4

Fig. 5

Quilt Class

The Liberated Log Cabin block is one of the most liberated of all liberated blocks. Be spontaneous!

- Start with a "squarish" center and frame it with strips of different widths.

- Begin with a traditional block as we did in *Pinwheels* or a liberated one as in *In Your Dreams*.

- Add more strips on one side than the other.

- Ignore any set formula for adding lights and darks.

Liberated Diagonal String Border

Appears in

Baskets with Sawtooth Handles (page 140)

Assembly

1. Cut long strips of assorted fabrics. Sew strips together along their long edges to make a strip set. Essentially, you are manufacturing "new" fabric. Press.

2. Place a 6" × 24" (15.2 cm × 61.0 cm) ruler on one corner of strip set at a 45-degree angle and cut off corner. Continue moving ruler along strip set at regular intervals to cut diagonal strips of desired width (fig. 1). We cut 4"-wide (10.2 cm) diagonal strips for *Baskets with Sawtooth Handles*.

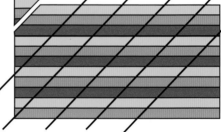

Fig. 1

3. Sew diagonal strips together to desired length (fig. 2). Press.

4. Square edges of strips (fig. 3).

Fig. 2

Fig. 3

Taking It from Tradition . . .

Strips may be cut to the same width for a uniform look. For a liberated effect (and a look more in keeping with antique quilts), cut strips in various widths (e.g., 1¼" [3.2 cm] to 3" [7.6 cm]).

Liberated Red Square

Appears in

Liberated Red Squares (page 160)

Cutting

For one block, cut:

▶ One red square 5" (12.7 cm) or 6" (15.2 cm)

▶ Assorted 1½" to 2½" (3.8 cm to 6.4 cm) × 5" (12.7 cm) strips

Assembly

1. Sew assorted strips into pairs, then fours, and so on until unit is long enough to sew to one side of red square (fig. 1). Make two.

Fig. 1

2. Sew units to side of square. Press. Repeat step 1 to make two additional units to fit remaining sides. Sew and press (figs. 2 and 3). Square block to desired size. The finished blocks in our quilt, *Liberated Red Squares*, measure approximately 11½" (29.2 cm) to 13" (33.0 cm).

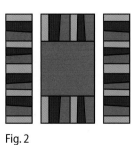

Fig. 2   Fig. 3

Quilt Class

For added "personality," vary the size of the center squares when you are making multiple blocks.

For an interesting alternative, substitute Diagonal String Blocks (page 86) or Liberated Diagonal String Borders (page 102) for some of the strip units (fig. 4).

Fig. 4

Liberated Star

Appears in

What a Star! (page 186)

Cutting

For each block, cut:

▶ Eight same-size background squares

▶ One square of same size from contrasting fabric

▶ Four squares slightly larger than background squares in same contrasting fabric, cut into eight half-square triangles

Assembly

1. With right sides together, position triangle on right side of background square. Before you sew, fold triangle back to make sure it will cover square completely. Sew triangle to square (fig. 1). Press triangle open from front side. Make four, shifting triangle slightly to vary points.

Fig. 1

2. Turn unit over and trim edges of triangle even with square (fig. 2). Turn unit over to front side and press again (fig. 3).

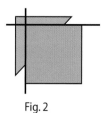

Fig. 2   Fig. 3

3. Repeat steps 1 and 2 to sew triangles to opposite side of unit. Press and trim.

4. Arrange units, remaining base squares, and same-size contrasting square and sew them into rows (fig. 4). Press.

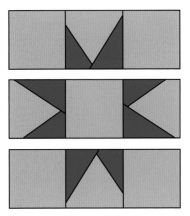

Fig. 4

5. Sew rows together (fig. 5). Press.

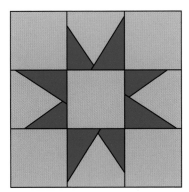

Fig. 5

Taking It from *Tradition* . . .

If you like, cut the center (contrasting) square from the background fabric as well.

Liberated Wedding Ring

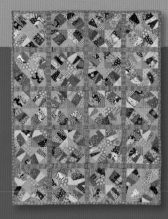

Appears in

Liberated Wedding Ring (page 162)

Cutting

For one 14"-square (35.6 cm) finished block, cut:

▶ Strips in various widths from assorted fabrics

▶ Four 5" (12.7 cm) squares from assorted fabrics in one color, cut into eight half-square triangles

Quilt Class

We used newspaper for the paper foundations. The paper was very easy to remove and made the whole process painless.

Assembly

1. Using pattern (fig. 1), cut four paper foundations.

2. Cover each paper foundation by sewing strips of assorted fabrics with "flip-and-sew" method. Trim fabric edges even with paper, but leave paper in place for now.

3. Sew triangles to opposite sides of each foundation-pieced unit (fig. 2). Press, and then square corners. Gently remove paper.

Fig. 2

4. Sew four units together (figs. 3 and 4). Press.

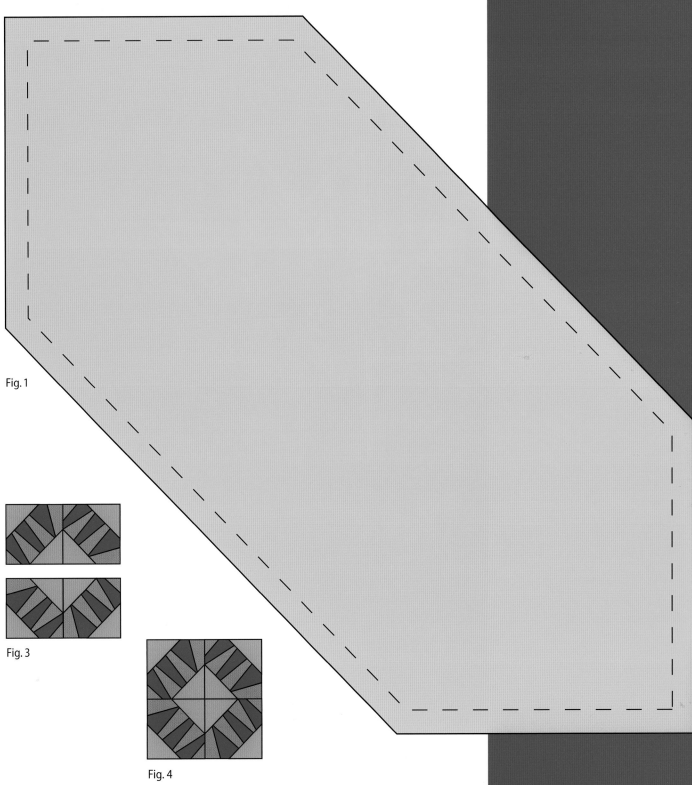

Fig. 1

Fig. 3

Fig. 4

Log Cabin Variation 1

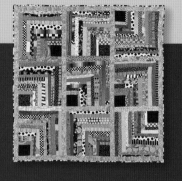

Appears in

House Top (page 154)

Cutting

For one 17"-square (43.2 cm) finished block, cut:

▶ One 5" (12.7 cm) corner square

▶ Strips in various widths from assorted fabrics

Assembly

1. Sew strips to adjacent sides of corner square, trimming as necessary (fig. 1). Press.

2. Repeat to sew second pair of strips to same sides (fig. 2). Press.

3. Continue sewing strips to same sides until block reaches desired size (fig. 3). Press.

Fig. 1

Fig. 2

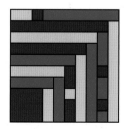

Fig. 3

Log Cabin Variation 11

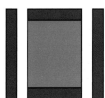

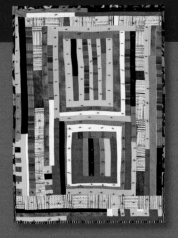

Appears in

Arbie's Quilt (page 136)
Around the Block (page 138)
Red and Green Triangles (page 178)

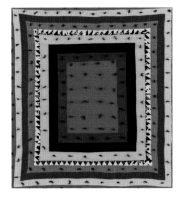

Cutting

For each block, cut:

▶ Center piece of desired size

▶ Strips in various widths from assorted fabrics

Assembly

1. Sew strips to opposite sides of center piece. Trim edges even with center piece. Press. Sew strips to remaining sides (fig. 1). Trim and press.

2. Repeat to sew second round of strips to unit (fig. 2). Trim and press.

3. Continue adding rounds of strips until your block has reached desired size (fig. 3).

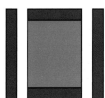

Fig. 1

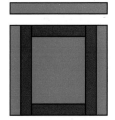

Fig. 2

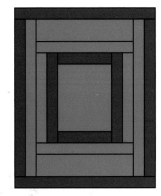

Fig. 3

Lone Star

Appears in

Lone Star (page 164)

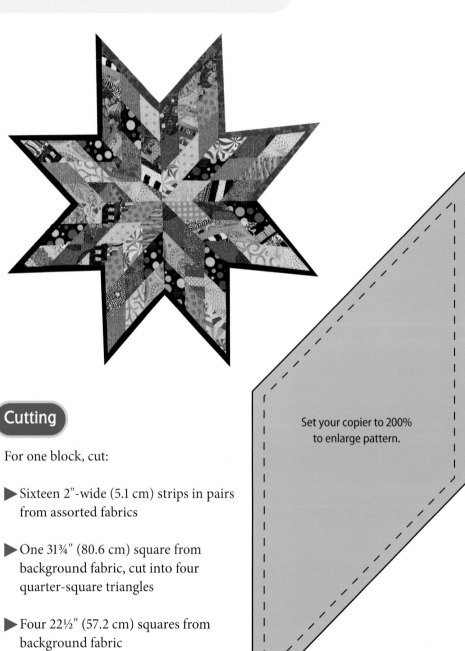

Cutting

For one block, cut:

▶ Sixteen 2"-wide (5.1 cm) strips in pairs from assorted fabrics

▶ One 31¾" (80.6 cm) square from background fabric, cut into four quarter-square triangles

▶ Four 22½" (57.2 cm) squares from background fabric

Set your copier to 200% to enlarge pattern.

Fig. 1

Assembly

1. Using pattern (fig. 1), make template.

2. Using template, cut seventy-two diamonds from assorted fabrics, either individually or by placing template on 4½"-wide (11.4 cm) strip (fig. 2).

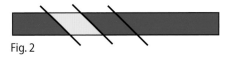

Fig. 2

3. Sew nine assorted diamonds together to make a large diamond (fig. 3). Press. Make eight.

Fig. 3

4. Sew matching strips to two adjoining sides of each large diamond (fig. 4). Trim and press.

Fig. 4

5. Sew large diamonds together in pairs, then fours, and then finally sew halves together (fig. 5). Press.

6. Set background triangles and squares into star unit (fig. 6). Press. Trim edges and square corners, leaving a generous seam allowance from diamond points to trimmed edges.

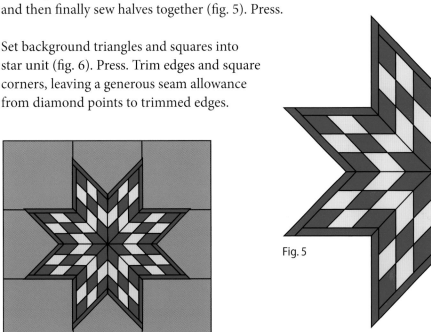

Fig. 5

Fig. 6

Nine Patch

Appears in

Definitely Gee's Bend (page 148)

Cutting

For multiple 3"-square (7.6 cm) finished units, cut:

▶ Three 1½" (3.8 cm) strips each of two contrasting colors

Assembly

1. Sew strips together along their long edges. Press. Make a strip set with one strip of one color between two strips of the other. Press. Cut into 1½"-wide (3.8 cm) segments (fig. 1).

Fig. 1

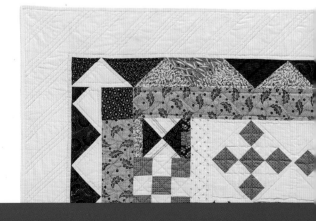

2. Reverse strip order for second strip set. Press. Cut into 1½"-wide (3.8 cm) segments (fig. 2).

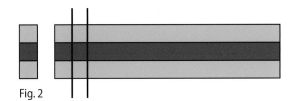

Fig. 2

3. Sew three segments together (figs. 3 and 4). Press.

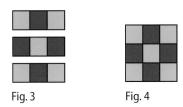

Fig. 3   Fig. 4

Taking It from Tradition . . .

Reverse the value placement for a different look (fig. 5). When making lots of these parts, cut strips in short lengths to guarantee a scrappy outcome. Just so you know: a 40"-long (101.6 cm) strip set yields about twenty-six 1½" (3.8 cm) segments.

Fig. 5

Our Garden

Appears in

Our Garden (page 168)

Cutting

For one 9"-square (22.9 cm) finished block, cut:

▶ Three 3⅞" (9.8 cm) squares from background fabric, cut into six small half-square triangles. You will use five.

▶ Two 3⅞" (9.8 cm) squares from contrasting fabric, cut into four small half-square triangles

▶ One 9⅞" (25.1 cm) square from a second contrasting fabric, cut into two large half-square triangles. You will use one.

Assembly

1. Sew small background and contrasting triangles together along their long edges (fig. 1). Press. Make three.

Fig. 1

2. Arrange and sew triangle units, two small background triangles, and one small contrasting triangle into rows. Press. Sew rows together. Press.

3. Sew unit from step 2 to large contrasting triangle along their long edges (fig. 2). Press.

Fig. 2

Pinwheel

Appears in

Pinwheels (page 170)

Cutting

For one 6"-square (15.2 cm) finished block, cut:

▶ Two 3⅞" (9.8 cm) squares from one fabric, cut into four half-square triangles

▶ Two 3⅞" (9.8 cm) squares from contrasting fabric, cut into four half-square triangles

Assembly

1. Sew one of each triangle together along their long edges (fig. 1). Press. Make four.

Fig. 1

2. Sew triangle units together (figs. 2 and 3). Press.

Fig. 2

Taking It from Tradition . . .

Rotate the triangles for a different look (fig. 4). If you wish, piece some of the triangles or cut them from Strata.

Fig. 4

Fig. 3

Posies

Appears in

Posies (page 172)

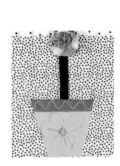  

Assembly

To make one block:

1. Cut strip of background fabric to desired width and length of finished block.

2. Freehand cut pot in size and shape you wish.

3. Place pot on background fabric. Cut background even with top of the pot (fig. 1). Set cut top background piece aside for now.

4. Shift pot slightly to left on background fabric and cut along right edge of pot (fig. 2).

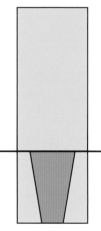

Fig. 1

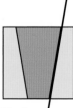

Fig. 2

5. Shift pot slightly to right and cut along left edge of pot (fig. 3).

6. Sew two background pieces to pot (fig. 4). Press.

7. Referring to Bias (Serpentine) Strips (page 84), make stem.

8. Using your preferred method, appliqué stem to background fabric you set aside in step 1 (fig. 5).

9. Join stem and pot sections. Press. Trim edges so they are even (fig. 6).

10. After quilt is quilted, make and add yo-yo posies (fig. 7). (See Yo-Yo, page 128.)

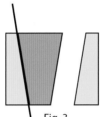

Fig. 3   Fig. 4

Fig. 5

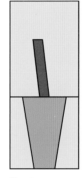

Fig. 6

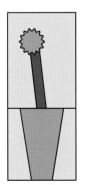

Fig. 7

Quilt Class

Our flower pot shapes vary in shape and some are even a little crooked. Make yours just the way you want them.

A bias strip is just one way to make the stem. If you prefer, freehand cut a curved piece, fuse it, and finish the edges with a hand or machine decorative stitch.

Make additional blocks in the same width so they can be sewn into vertical rows. The length of the block doesn't matter.

Pyramid

Appears in

Pyramids (page 174)

Assembly

1. Using pattern (fig. 1), make a template.

2. Using template, cut triangles from mix of colors, values, and prints.

3. Arrange one row of triangles, making sure there is contrast from triangle to triangle, and alternating their direction. Sew triangles together to complete row (fig. 2). Press.

Fig. 2

4. Make desired number of rows.

5. Arrange rows "head to toe." Sew rows together. Press. Trim side edges (fig. 3).

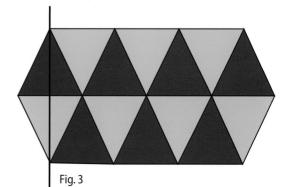

Fig. 3

Fig. 1

Spider Web

Appears in

Spider Web (page 182)

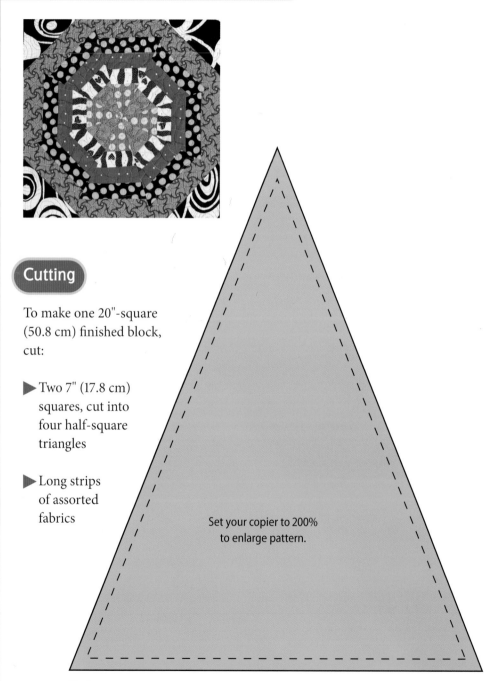

Cutting

To make one 20"-square (50.8 cm) finished block, cut:

▶ Two 7" (17.8 cm) squares, cut into four half-square triangles

▶ Long strips of assorted fabrics

Set your copier to 200% to enlarge pattern.

Fig. 1

Assembly

1. Sew strips together randomly along their long edges until total width equals about 12" (30.5 cm). Press seams flat.

2. Using pattern (fig. 1), make a template.

3. Place template on new "fabric" and cut eight triangles, rotating template for each new triangle (fig. 2).

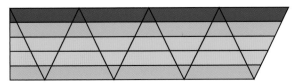

Fig. 2

4. Arrange triangles so inner and outer colors alternate (fig. 3). Sew triangles together in pairs, then fours, and finally sew halves together. Sew triangles to corners (fig. 4). Press, and then square corners.

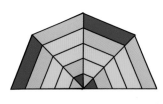

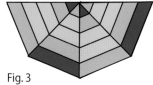

Fig. 3

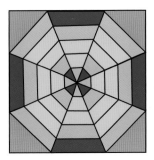

Fig. 4

Quilt Class

We think this block has more personality when the strips are cut in varying widths; for example, from 1¼" (3.2 cm) to 3" (7.6 cm) wide.

To make a nine-block quilt, make eight strip sets. Each strip set yields nine wedges, so you'll have enough left over from each strip set to make the ninth block.

Spike

Appears in

Spikes (page 184)

Cutting

For "traditional" spikes, cut:

▶ An equal number of same-size rectangles from two contrasting fabrics

Assembly

1. Cut rectangles diagonally from top left to bottom right (fig. 1). You must cut all rectangles in same direction. It will not work if you cut some one way and others another way.

2. Sew one triangle of each fabric together along their long diagonal edges (fig. 2). Press (fig. 3).

3. Make additional units and sew them together (fig. 4). Press.

Fig. 1

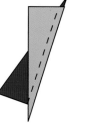

Fig. 2

Fig. 3

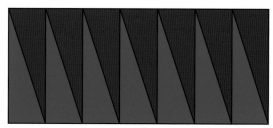

Fig. 4

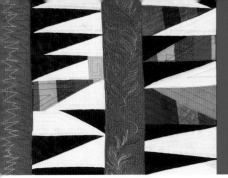

Cutting

For liberated spikes, cut:

▶ One 4½"-wide (11.4 cm) strip from background fabric

▶ Assorted 3" × 5½" (7.6 cm × 14.0 cm) rectangles from contrasting fabrics

Assembly

1. Cut background strip into even or uneven segments, depending upon how liberated you want your spikes to be.

2. Cut contrasting rectangles diagonally from corner to corner. You must cut all rectangles in same direction. It will not work if you cut some one way and others another way.

3. With right sides together, position triangle on right side of rectangle. Before you sew, fold triangle back to make sure it will cover rectangle completely. Sew triangle to rectangle (fig. 5). Press triangle open from front side.

Fig. 5

4. Turn unit over and trim edges of triangle even with rectangle (fig. 6). Turn unit over to front side and press again (fig. 7).

5. Make additional units and sew them together (fig. 8). Place triangles at slightly different angles to create liberated effect.

Fig. 6

Fig. 7

Fig. 8

Sticks

Appears in

In Your Dreams (page 156)
Red Sticks (page 180)

 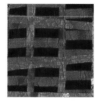 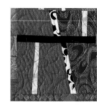

Cutting

To make one block, cut:

▶ One 8"-wide (20.3 cm) piece of red fabric

▶ Two or three 1"-wide (2.5 cm) (approximate) strips of contrasting fabric(s)

Assembly

1. Slice red piece at several different angles (figs. 1 and 2).

2. Insert strips as you sew piece back together (figs. 3 and 4). Trim strips as needed. Press.

3. Trim block to desired width and length.

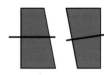

Fig. 1   Fig. 2

Fig. 3   Fig. 4

Strata

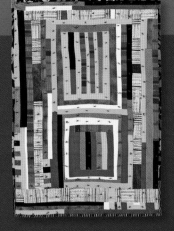

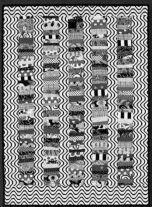

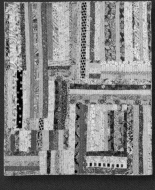

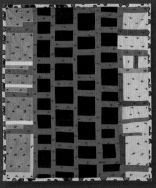

Appears in

Arbie's Quilt (page 136)
Chinese Coins (page 144)
Garden Path (page 150)
Marzella's Quilt (page 166)

Assembly

1. Cut long strips of assorted fabrics. Sew strips together along their long edges to make a strip set. Essentially, you are "manufacturing" new fabric. Press.

2. Cut new "fabric" into segments of desired widths or shapes. For *Chinese Coins*, we cut segments 6" (15.2 cm) wide (fig. 1). For *Arbie's Quilt* and *Garden Path*, we used large sections of uncut Strata.

3. Sew segments together to achieve desired length.

Fig. 1

String-Pieced Basket

Appears in

Beautiful Baskets (page 142)

Cutting

For one 14"-square (35.6 cm) finished block, cut:

▶ One 3⅞" (9.8 cm) square from background fabric, cut into two small half-square triangles

▶ One 11⅞" (30.2 cm) square from background fabric, cut into two large half-square triangles. You will use one.

▶ Two 3½" × 8½" (8.9 cm × 21.6 cm) rectangles from background fabric

▶ One 3½" (8.9 cm) square from background fabric

▶ One 3⅞" (9.8 cm) square from contrasting (basket) fabric, cut into two small half-square triangles

Assembly

1. There are two ways to piece the basket base: Cut one 11⅞" (30.2 cm) square from newspaper; cut into two large half-square triangles. You will use one. Use "flip-and-sew" method to cover paper triangle with fabric strips of assorted widths. Trim fabric edges even with edges of paper triangle (fig. 1).
OR
Make strip set using fabric strips ranging from 1¼" (3.2 cm) to 3" (7.6 cm) wide. Press. Cut strip set to make one 11⅞" (30.2 cm) square; cut into two large half-square triangles (fig. 1). You will use one.

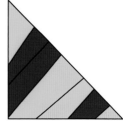

Fig. 1

2. Sew small background and basket triangles together (fig. 2). Press. Make two.

Fig. 2

3. Referring to Bias (Serpentine) Strips (page 84), make basket handle.

4. Using your preferred method, appliqué handle to large background triangle.

5. Arrange string-pieced basket unit, appliquéd triangle, two background rectangles, two small triangle units, and background square (fig. 3). Sew basket unit and appliquéd triangle together. Press. Sew rectangles and triangle units together. Press. Sew one rectangle/triangle unit to left edge of block. Press. Sew 3½" (8.9 cm) square to remaining rectangle/triangle unit. Press and sew to bottom edge of the block (fig. 4). Press.

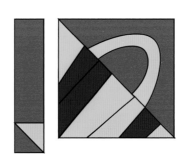

Fig. 3

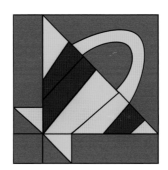

Fig. 4

Quilt Class

A bias strip is just one way to make the handle. If you prefer, freehand cut a curved piece, fuse it, and finish the edges with a hand or machine decorative stitch.

Yo-Yo

Appears in

Posies (page 172)

Assembly

1. Cut circle from desired fabric. Turn under raw edge of circle ¼" (0.3 cm) to wrong side and baste using single strand of knotted thread (fig. 1). Do not cut thread.

Fig. 1

2. Gather thread to pull turned raw edges together to form right-side-out "pouch" (fig. 2).

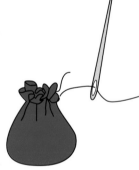

Fig. 2

3. Smooth and flatten pouch into circle (fig. 3). Secure to quilt as desired.

Fig. 3

Chapter 5

48" × 58" (121.9 cm × 147.3 cm) ▪ 2006

Our Collaborative Work: Everything Old Is New Again

$\mathcal{S}$ ince our first book, *Collaborative Quilting*, was published we've heard from many quilters that they were more than a little shocked to learn that the two of us were collaborating. For some reason, they thought it was odd that two people with "nothing in common" actually would consider working together.

Friends

Now that we are older, we can dress ourselves, and that's what we did in this second self-portrait. (You can see the first on the cover of our first book, *Collaborative Quilting*.) Can you guess which is Freddy and which is Gwen? Hints might include the color of our apparel and the fact that one "chick" is pigeon-toed.

How (and Why) We Collaborate

While two people who make the same style of quilt might find it easier to work together, we found that it is our differences that added a unique richness to our collaborative work. We discovered that the benefit of working with someone who comes to the table with a completely different point of view resulted in our making quilts that probably neither of us would have made on our own.

The very fact that we were so different made for some challenges along the way, but it was the very thing that made it interesting and exciting for both of us. It also pushed each of us out of our comfort zones and headlong into trying things we might not otherwise have explored.

As both of us are sure-footed, independent women, we had to set some guidelines and devise a framework to steer our new enterprise. This was the first thing we did when Freddy initially brought up the possibility of collaboration. An obvious solution was that we should both play from our strong points. When you think of Freddy Moran, you think of exuberant color; it is what she is known for most, so it was natural she should take on that part of the process. Gwen is a long-time student of quilting history and tradition and has been teaching and writing about her liberated quiltmaking techniques since 1991. Her classes are always about designing original work, so she became the designer. These two decisions, coupled with the fact that we both are willing to entertain all ideas and try just about anything, has made our collaboration a success, not to mention fun, and we think that's reflected in our work.

■ What You'll Find in These Pages

The following pages are brimming with colorful quilts, each a marriage of tradition and innovation. While we certainly encourage you to enjoy the visuals, we also hope you will take the time to study the information that accompanies each luscious photo.

Along with each quilt, you'll find information describing:

- The parts that we used to make the quilt.

- A list of additional materials involved in making that quilt—backing, binding fabric, batting, and so on.

- Background on the source of inspiration and/or how the design evolved.

- Special design elements to look for and to emulate in your own quilts.

Whenever possible, we've also included a link to a traditional block or technique to show you the strong connection between our quilts and their 19th- and early 20th-century roots. We hope that these examples open your eyes to the many ways and many colorways in which our Parts Department can be used.

A Word from Gwen

As the designer in our collaboration, I obviously rely on what I know about quilts, and what I know about quilts I've learned from studying antique examples. Certain artistic concepts from antique quilts have long played an important role in my own work. While these concepts were common in 19th-century quilts, they have—for the most part—been eradicated from today's quilts. Here is a summary of ideas from our quilting predecessors that we have used in our collaborative work:

- Simple pieced patterns (e.g., One Patch, Four Patch, Nine Patch, Log Cabin)

- Pieced patches

- Asymmetrical design

- Random color placement

- Color substitution

- No corner resolution on borders

- Shapes cut directly from fabric (no templates)

- Four-block settings

- Tied quilts

- Edges finished by bringing the backing to the front and topstitching it in place

- Less emphasis on precision

A final word about precision: I've never understood what seems to be the over-preoccupation with precision in the quilt world. It seems to me that the making of art has very little to do with staying inside the lines.

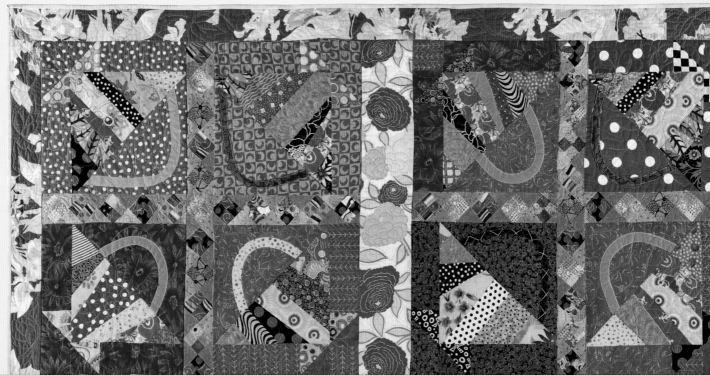

1937 Revisited

This quilt utilizes a four-block-in-a-four-block format. The idea for this quilt originated with a vintage 1937 quilt block. How contemporary!

From The Parts Department

Diagonal String Block (page 86)

In addition to the parts, you will need:

- Backing fabric
- Basic tool kit
- Batting
- Binding fabric
- Two different fabrics for sashing

Strata is a fancy new word for what we generally call "making new fabric." To create the blocks for this eye-catching quilt, we sewed together alternating plain and pieced strips in varying widths to create a wide Strata. Next, we cut blocks on the diagonal and set them with a bold black-and-white polka dot sashing to define the four-block units and to add sparkle. The stark black sashing that runs vertically and horizontally through the center adds drama to the overall design, a simple composition with powerful results.

Look Closely: Design Highlights

- Sixteen blocks, each 11½" (29.2 cm) square finished (Strata approximately 17" [43.2 cm] wide)
- Two different sashing fabrics, each one cut to a different width
- No border; not every quilt needs one

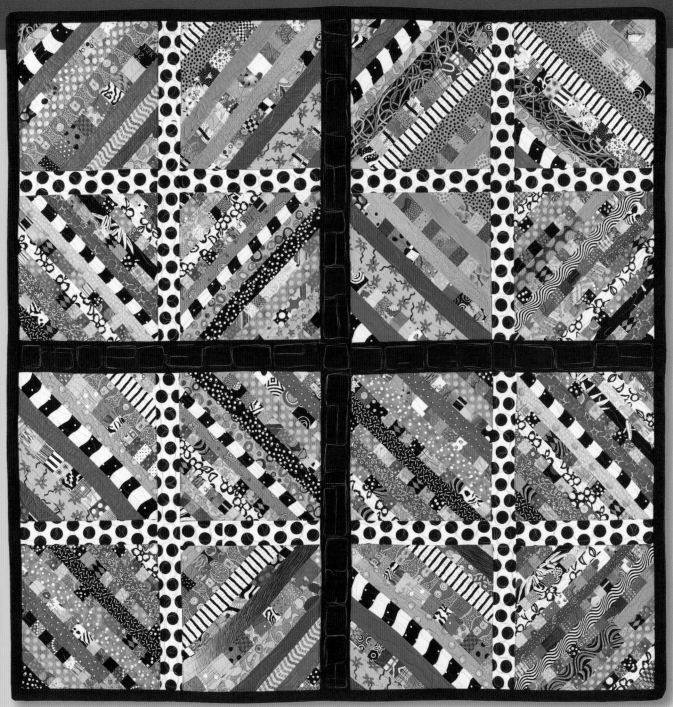

55" × 55" (139.7 cm × 139.7 cm) ▪ 2006

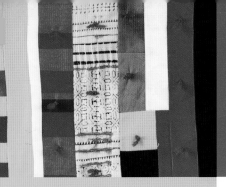

Arbie's Quilt

We discovered the inspiration for this quilt in a catalogue for a 1998 exhibit at the South Carolina State Museum in Columbia. It was made by Arbie Williams, who was born in Carthage, Texas, in 1916. Arbie called her quilt *Banana Split*. Our version includes fabric from Africa and Southeast Asia, which seem quite at home in this hand-tied piece.

From The Parts Department

Log Cabin Variation II (page 109)
Strata (page 125)

In addition to the parts, you will need:

- Backing fabric
- Basic tool kit
- Batting
- Wool for tying

For *Arbie's Quilt*, we paired an interesting textured denim from Thailand with a group of solid-colored damasks from the African nation of Chad. (The vibrant colors were too good to resist!) The weave of the damasks made them somewhat difficult to work with, but they were perfect for the casual style of the quilt. You wouldn't, however, want to use them to piece a Feathered Star.

We were both attracted to the idea of making some tied quilts, a long out-of-fashion alternative to quilting. We tied this quilt with wool and finished the edges with a traditional Amish-style binding, described in The Back-To-Front Method on page 75, so a healthy slice of the pieced backing fabrics shows.

Look Closely: Design Highlights

- Mix of unusual fabrics from different sources
- Pieced backing
- Tying as an alternative for securing the layers of hard-to-quilt fabrics
- Rollover binding (back to front)

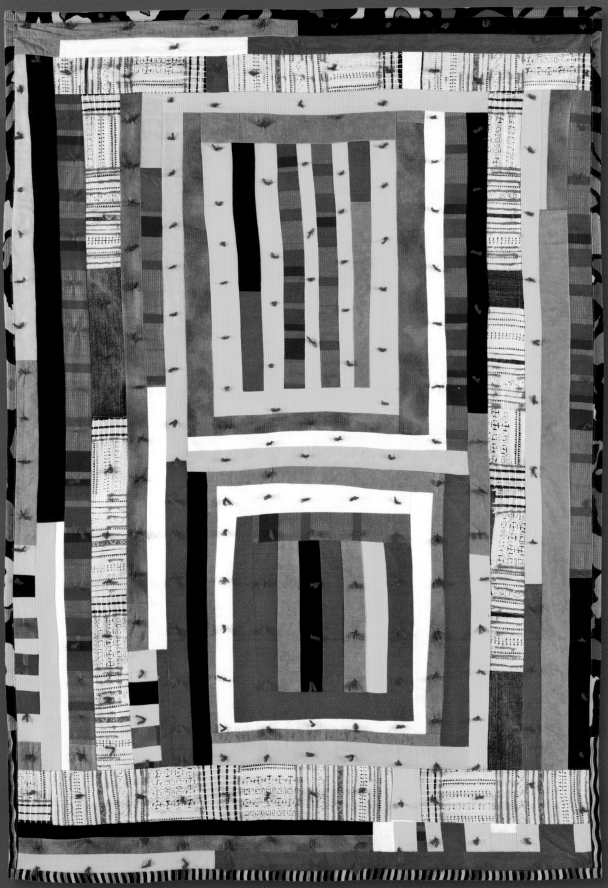

41" × 58" (104.1 cm × 147.3 cm) ▪ 2007

Around the Block

The amazing quilts of Arbie Williams continue to inspire us. We discovered her quilt, named simply *Medallion*, in Eli Leon's book, *Who'd a Thought It: Improvisations in African-American Quiltmaking*. (See Bibliography, page 189). That quilt became the inspiration for our collaborative effort.

From The Parts Department

Half-Square-Triangle Unit (page 94)
Log Cabin Variation II (page 109)

In addition to the parts, you will need:

- Backing fabric
- Basic tool kit
- Batting
- Wool for tying

We had a blast making tied quilts for this book. At the same time, we were enjoying the design concepts of the Gee's Bend and other African-American quilts, and the elements seemed perfectly matched.

Like the original that inspired us, this particular quilt is made in the medallion style, using ever-popular collaborative quilter damask solids. The key to the composition is the change in value from "frame" to "frame," and the introduction of the unexpected Sawtooth borders.

Once again, we tied the quilt with wool and finished the edges by turning the back to front, topstitching the "binding" in place.

Tradition . . .

Detail of **Pennsylvania Sampler**, c. 1890–1910: Same idea, just on a smaller scale. This wonderful block, made about 100 years ago, shares many elements of construction and design with **Around the Block**.

Look Closely: Design Highlights

Sawtooth borders cut to fit

Outer borders broken with strips running in the opposite direction

Tying as an alternative to quilting

Rollover binding (back to front)

58" × 63" (147.3 cm × 160.0 cm) ▪ 2007

Baskets with Sawtooth Handles

The scale of the block (20" [50.8 cm]) is a huge factor in the design of the quilt.

From The Parts Department

Basket with Sawtooth Handle (page 82)
Liberated Diagonal String Border (page 102)

In addition to the parts, you will need:

- Backing fabric
- Basic tool kit
- Batting
- Binding fabric
- Two different fabrics for sashing

Gwen got the idea for the handles from a circa 1850 quilt, and our collaborative version grew from there. Since she is much more proficient making handles, she made them all by folding the fabrics and cutting the shapes by eye, which gives the end result a joyous freedom. Freddy contributed the exuberant color scheme and pieced the basket bottoms. Compare the colors of this quilt with the more traditional palette Gwen chose for *Baskets with Dog Tooth Handles* (page 18).

After we assembled the blocks to make the quilt center, we went to our handy Parts Department and found the Liberated Diagonal String Border just waiting to frame this quilt.

The use of so many different yellows for the background adds depth and interest and takes this quilt from ordinary to "wow!" while the repetition of the red and blue handles keeps things under reasonable control.

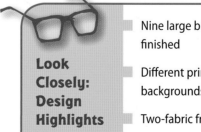

Look Closely: Design Highlights

Nine large blocks, each 20" (50.8 cm) square finished

Different prints in the same color family for block backgrounds, even within the same block

Two-fabric freehand-cut handles

Try this: We didn't here, but you can fill the baskets with appliqué

68" × 68" (172.7 cm × 172.7 cm) ▪ 2006

Beautiful Baskets

This contemporary quilt owes its concept to two very traditional ideas: the string-pieced block and the four-block setting. Both have a special place in the history of the American quilt. As the author of a book on each subject, Gwen is quite familiar with these two types of quilts, and so she was right at home devising this design.

From The Parts Department

Bias (Serpentine) Strips (page 84)
Four Patch (page 92)
String-Pieced Basket (page 126)

In addition to the parts, you will need:

- Backing fabric
- Basic tool kit
- Batting
- Binding fabric
- Border fabric
- Sashing fabric (for center sashing)
- Sashing fabric (for on-point setting triangles)

Here is another example of the traditional use-it-up technique of string piecing. We created triangular foundations from newspaper, and covered them with strips and strings of bright, knock-your-socks-off prints. (You may recognize Freddy's "red is a neutral" contribution in the powerful background fabrics.) The curved handles provide a nice counterpoint for the busy geometry of the overall quilt.

We complemented the traditional four-blocks-in-four-blocks setting by including small-scale, on-point Four Patch blocks in the first round of sashing strips; the combination of red and turquoise turned out to be a stunner. The second round of sashing, cut from a lighter, large-scale print, seemed to advance toward our eyes, giving the two-dimensional surface the illusion of depth.

Tradition . . .

Detail of *Sampler*, c. 1890–1910: It doesn't take much imagination to see the connection between this vintage Basket block and the baskets in our quilt. We swapped out the triangle base for a string-pieced alternative, but the basic shape and handle are very much the same.

Look Closely: Design Highlights

- Sixteen basket blocks, each 14" (35.6 cm) square finished
- Four-patch parts finish 2" (5.1 cm) square
- Different prints in the same color family for block backgrounds, even within the same block
- Sashing fabrics differ in value to create a three-dimensional effect
- Try this: Cut basket bases from Strata as an alternative to foundation piecing

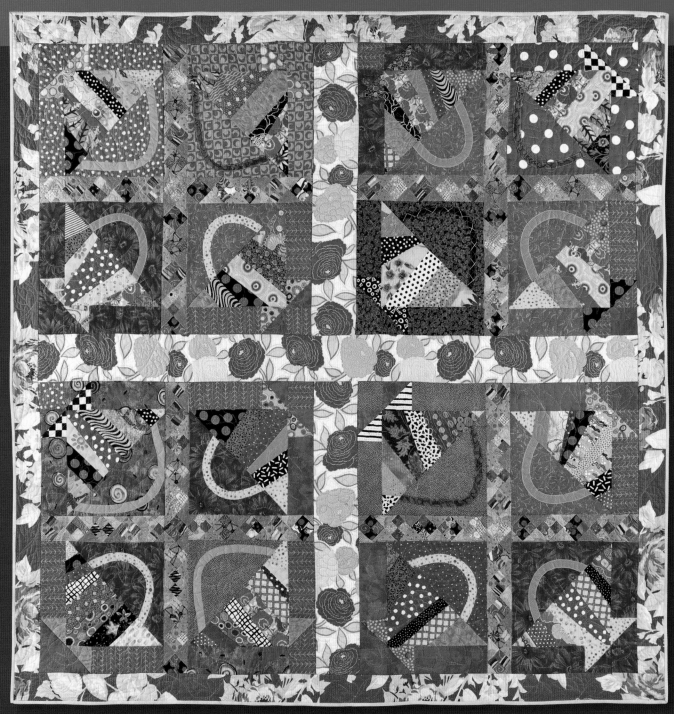

71" × 71" (180.3 cm × 180.3 cm) ▪ 2006

Chinese Coins

This is a simple, classic pattern made all the more interesting by the use of uneven strips and no discernable formula for placing the fabrics.

From The Parts Department

Strata (page 125)

In addition to the parts, you will need:

- Backing fabric
- Basic tool kit
- Batting
- Binding fabric
- Sashing and border fabric

We have both admired traditional Chinese Coins quilts and decided to make a Gwen and Freddy version, so as our foremothers did before us, we dug into our scraps. One of the beauties of a vertically oriented quilt is that only one measurement needs to be consistent—the length of the rows. The rows (and the strips within them) can be cut to random widths. The trick was to keep the quilt looking scrappy—that is, with no predictable formula or repetition of fabrics—and we feel we were successful. Notice the wavy black-and-white setting fabric. It does the trick, doesn't it?

Look Closely: Design Highlights

- Five pieced rows, 5½" (14.0 cm) wide finished
- Strips within the rows vary in width
- Fabulous fabric used for sashing repeated in the borders; pieced rows seem to float
- Try this: Vary widths of pieced rows or even width of sashing in between

51" × 65" (129.5 cm × 165.1 cm) ▪ 2007

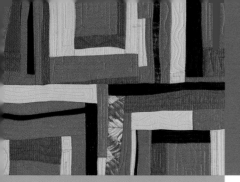

Damask Log Cabin

Inspiration for a quilt can come from anywhere: a photo, artwork in other media, fabric. In this case, once we had the fabulous fabric in hand, this quilt just designed itself.

From The Parts Department

Liberated Log Cabin (page 100)

In addition to the parts, you will need:

- Backing fabric
- Basic tool kit
- Batting
- Binding fabric
- Border fabric

Freddy found the fabric for this quilt in an artifact shop of ethnic treasures in Northern California. The fabric comes from a small village in Africa where it is hand dyed to surprisingly intense saturations of color. We fell in love not only with the colors, but with the way the textured surface of the damask showcased the dyes for fabulous color-on-color effects.

Tradition . . .

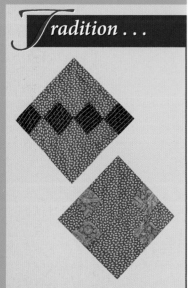

Detail of *Four Patch*, c. 1910–1920: Blurring the boundaries within the blocks, and between blocks and backgrounds, is nothing new. Sarah Gruber Replage did it in her quilt almost 100 years ago. You can too!

Look Closely: Design Highlights

- Fifteen blocks in varying sizes
- Setting built in horizontal rows
- Unequal number of blocks in rows
- Use of border fabric in blocks—particularly in outer strips—blurs the boundaries between blocks and border

63" × 73" (160.0 cm × 185.4 cm) ▪ 2008

Definitely Gee's Bend

We discovered in our research that the ladies of Gee's Bend used lots and lots of Flying Geese in their quilts, sometimes using them for the entire quilt top.

From The Parts Department

Flying Geese (page 90)
Nine Patch (page 112)

In addition to the parts, you will need:

- Backing fabric
- Basic tool kit
- Batting
- Binding fabric
- Border fabric (for on-point setting triangles)
- Sashing fabric

After hours of poring over books about the Gee's Bend quilts and quilters, we decided to adopt a similar approach for this quilt. Using the complementary colors of red and green made both colors appear more vibrant. We cut bright red sashing strips, varying the widths to compensate for variations in the size of the Flying Geese sections, and added an on-point Nine Patch border on three sides, making for a very lively, and somewhat unpredictable, quilt. We must admit, though, we were finished with Flying Geese for a while after piecing this sweetheart.

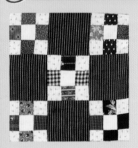

Detail of *Pennsylvania Sampler*, c. 1890–1910: The Nine Patch block appears in one form or another in many sampler quilts. It was often the first block a young girl was taught to stitch. Compare the colors and arrangement of these Nine Patches with the bright on-point version in the borders of our quilt.

Look Closely: Design Highlights

Six large sections vary in size

Sashing strips cut in different widths to help sections "fit"

Placement of value changes in some Flying Geese

Some rows "fly" in the opposite direction

Pieced borders on three sides only

65" × 83" (165.1 cm × 210.8 cm) ▪ 2006

Garden Path

Ararity for our collaborative work—and especially shocking for Freddy—this quilt uses no black-and-white fabrics.

From The Parts Department

Strata (page 125)

In addition to the parts, you will need:

- Backing fabric
- Basic tool kit
- Batting
- Binding fabric

We stitched a wide variety of prints in a largely pastel palette to make this scrappy quilt, similar in its construction and design sensibility to many vintage utility quilts. We sewed strips of varying widths together to make Strata, which we then re-cut and assembled freeform on the design wall. It's a perfect example of simple, intuitive design, the hallmark of many antique scrap quilts.

Look Closely: Design Highlights

Some Strata are placed horizontally, some vertically for added movement

Some individual strips are pieced

A few high-contrast fabrics (in color, value, or intensity) add depth

Binding made from a striped fabric cut (or printed) on the bias

56" × 65" (142.2 cm × 165.1 cm) ▪ 2007

Gee's Bend a la California

This began as a two-color quilt until "someone" couldn't stand it any longer and added a multicolored print. We wonder who…

From The Parts Department

Gee's Bend a la California (page 93)
Half-Square-Triangle Unit (page 94)

In addition to the parts, you will need:

- Backing fabric
- Basic tool kit
- Batting
- Binding fabric

This is another quilt inspired by the Gee's Bend quilters. It is constructed in units made with half-square triangles, and assembled in six vertical panels. Some blocks are turned sideways or even upside down; this visual interruption in the expected flow of the quilt creates wonderful "surprises" throughout the design. The startling red and turquoise color scheme is a major design element.

Look Closely: Design Highlights

- A scattering of one larger-scale, multicolored print
- Occasional parts (or groups of parts) change direction
- "Parts of parts" and filler strips fill in the gaps

51" × 59" (129.5 cm × 149.9 cm) ▪ 2006

House Top

Even in what may appear at first to be chaotic, there are constants that pull this design together: the repeating block, the border fabric, and a healthy sprinkling of black-and-white prints.

From The Parts Department

Log Cabin Variation I (page 108)

In addition to the parts, you will need:

- Assorted fabrics for horizontal sashing
- Backing fabric
- Basic tool kit
- Batting
- Binding fabric
- Fabric for vertical sashing and border

Takeoffs on the Log Cabin block are legion. One reason the design has been (and remains) so popular is that it doesn't require a pattern. Anyone could make it … and so they did.

This rather loud quilt utilizes just one of the many Log Cabin arrangements. We started with a square, and then added strips from our scrap bag in a very casual manner on two sides only until the blocks were all approximately the same size. Next we squared them all to measure 18" × 18" (45.7 cm × 45.7 cm).

Note that the strips we used for the blocks are of random width, even within the same block. This is quite a discovery. One might ask, "Why would *anyone* sew those two pieces of fabric together?" Our response? "Why? Because more is more!"

We sewed the blocks into vertical rows and separated the rows with sashing cut from a large-scale, pink cabbage rose print that we used again to frame the quilt. Once again, we used black-and-white fabrics to keep the eye traveling across the surface.

Look Closely: Design Highlights

- Nine blocks, each approximately 18" (45.7 cm) square finished
- Some strips are straight, and some are not
- Some strips are pieced to achieve the desired length

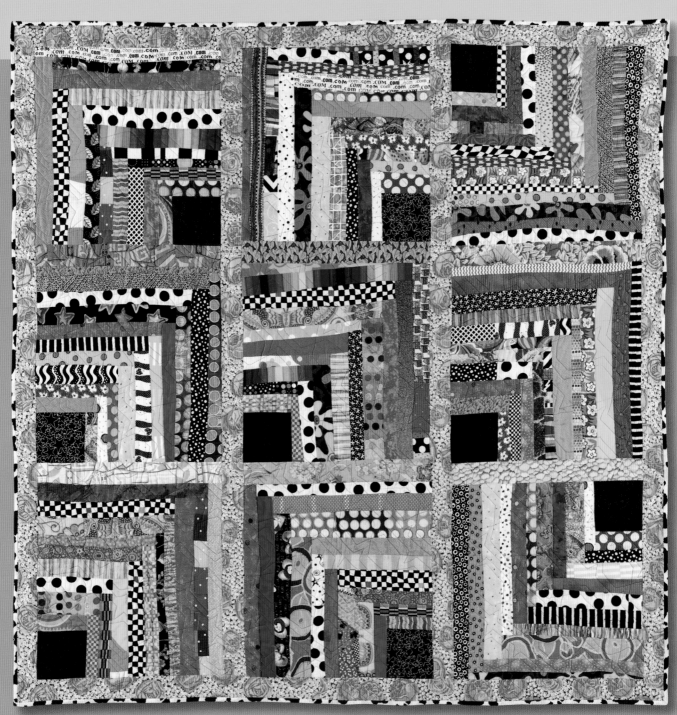

60" × 60" (152.4 cm × 152.4 cm) ▪ 2006

In Your Dreams

The quirky figured fabric had been in Gwen's stash awaiting an exciting application … and here it is. The challenge then was to find suitable setting fabrics, and boy, were we successful!

From The Parts Department

Bias (Serpentine) Strips (page 84)
Liberated House (page 98)
Liberated Log Cabin (page 100)
Sticks (page 124)

In addition to the parts, you will need:

- Backing fabric
- Basic tool kit
- Batting
- Binding fabric
- Border fabric
- Sashing fabric

We had a limited quantity of the focus fabric for this quilt and wanted to use every figure. We cut each one carefully to the same height so we could sew them into rows. (Don't you love the cut-off heads? It appears to us that these little men are walking behind billboards.) We made the separating strips in different widths and used them in a combined Liberated House and Log Cabin fashion in keeping with the "personality" of the quilt. Then, as luck would have it, we found the perfect border fabric.

Look Closely: Design Highlights

Serpentine strips finish 1¼" (3.2 cm) wide

Parts are combined to make new blocks (Liberated Log Cabin and Liberated House)

Parts used as fillers (Sticks)

No, it's not appliqué; the border print does the work

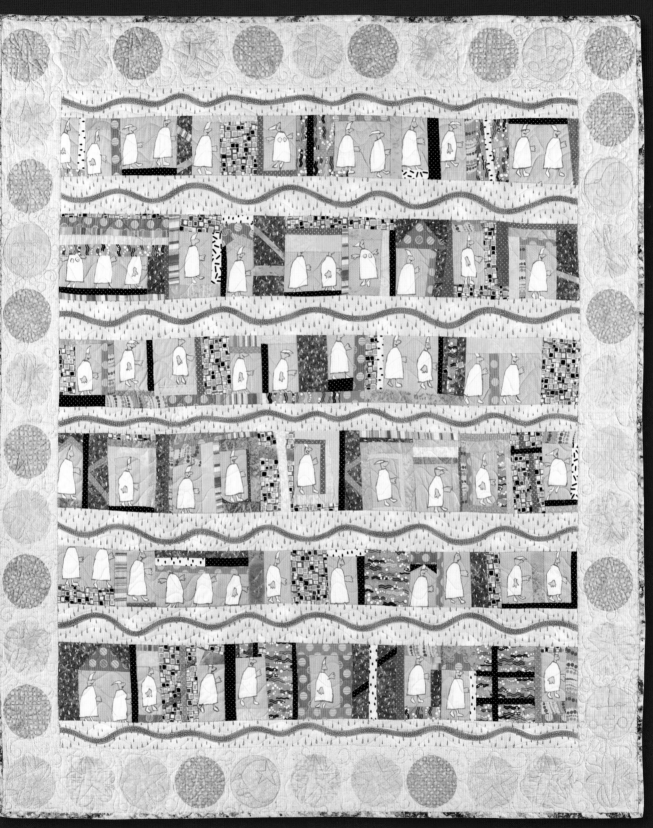

61" × 71" (154.9 cm × 180.3 cm) ▪ 2006

It's All About Triangles

Many of these Half-Square-Triangle Units had been waiting patiently in our Parts Department since 2003. It was time to put them to work.

From The Parts Department

Half-Square-Triangle Unit (page 94)

In addition to the parts, you will need:

- Backing fabric
- Basic tool kit
- Batting
- Binding fabric
- Sashing fabric

Starting with the medallion format and lots of Half-Square-Triangle Units from The Parts Department, we built this quilt from the center out, adapting the size of the units "on the fly" as we added each border. As you can see, we used many different sizes of triangle units. Inserting an occasional black-and-white border—pieced or not—made the transitions from round to round easier to read.

Look Closely: Design Highlights

The same part is repeated in various (finished) sizes: 1½" (3.8 cm), 3" (7.6 cm), 4" (10.2 cm), 5½" (14.0 cm)

Half-Square-Triangle Units turn every which way

Rows are cut off mid-triangle to fit

Parts go from medium, to larger, to small, and back to large again

A single unpieced border gives the eye a place to rest

58" × 58" (147.3 cm × 147.3 cm) ▪ 2006

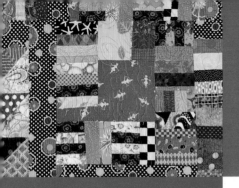

Liberated Red Squares

As evidenced by many vintage scrappy quilts, our grandmothers felt free to substitute if they ran short and had a different block handy. When we came up short on this quilt, we followed suit. We firmly believe it's these little surprises that lift a quilt out of the ordinary.

From The Parts Department

Diagonal String Block (page 86)
Diamond Border (page 88)
Half-Square-Triangle Unit (page 94)
Liberated Red Square (page 103)

In addition to the parts, you will need:

- Backing fabric
- Basic tool kit
- Batting
- Binding fabric

For this quilt, we created Strata (see page 125), which we cut and stitched Log Cabin-style around squares cut in slightly different sizes from a variety of bright red prints. Then we began to arrange the blocks in rows, but—oops!—the rows were not all the same length and we had run out of Liberated Red Square blocks. Did that stop us? No way! We raided The Parts Department to fill in the gaps as needed.

The namesake red squares unify the design and invite the viewer to discover the unexpected elements that spice up what might otherwise have been a rather predictable (read: boring) quilt. And what an exciting border! Slight variations, particularly in the values of the red and green prints, emphasize the movement in this already lively border motif.

radition . . .

Detail of
Pennsylvania Sampler, c. 1890–1910: We didn't invent the idea of cutting off or cutting up blocks to fill out uneven rows. This quilter did it with great panache!

Look Closely: Design Highlights

- Nineteen blocks vary from 11½" (29.2 cm) to 13" (33.0 cm) square finished
- Some Strata replaced with Diagonal String blocks
- Filler strips and other parts even out the rows
- Similar (but different) red and green prints in the border

66" × 84" (167.6 cm × 213.4 cm) ▪ 2006

Liberated Wedding Ring

This quilt draws its up-to-the-minute look from Freddy's selection of bright, colorful fabrics and the scale of the blocks. It's a "modern" version of Gwen's *Liberated Wedding Ring* (page 27), which she made with more traditional, reproduction fabrics.

From The Parts Department

Liberated Wedding Ring (page 106)

In addition to the parts, you will need:

- Backing fabric
- Basic tool kit
- Batting
- Binding fabric
- Sashing fabric

The charm of this Wedding Ring variation is in its repetition of shape and color. In time-honored fashion, we used newspaper foundations to string piece the lozenge shapes for the rings, and created a "background" by using assorted orange prints throughout for the corner triangles.

The blocks are set in a traditional format with vertical and horizontal sashing, once again in a graphic black-and-white stripe. This bold print, which Freddy thinks gives the eye a place to rest, defines the block and prevents the quilt from becoming a "big orange mush." We could have stopped at a smaller size, but we loved the design so much, we just kept going.

Tradition . . .

Detail of *Pennsylvania Sampler*, c. 1890–1910: There are echoes of our *Liberated Wedding Ring* in the center of this block, also called Single Wedding Ring by some. The resemblance is even more striking in Gwen's version on page 27.

Look Closely: Design Highlights

- Twenty blocks, each 14" (35.6 cm) square finished
- Bold color and fabric choices for corner triangles, sashing, and binding
- Try this: Instead of foundation piecing, cut "rings" from Strata

61" × 77" (154.9 cm × 195.6 cm) ▪ 2006

Lone Star

For this scrappy quilt, we didn't match the diamonds, but let them mingle freely, giving this quilt the look of a party in full swing.

From The Parts Department

Lone Star (page 110)

In addition to the parts, you will need:
- Backing fabric
- Basic tool kit
- Batting
- Binding fabric
- Fabric for setting triangles and squares
- Two different fabrics for outlining star points

We played it very loose with this quilt to create a bold version of the much-loved traditional quilt pattern. Eight large diamonds, each consisting of nine smaller diamonds, make up the large star, which we framed with 1½"-wide (3.8 cm) finished strips for added emphasis.

Based on our color choices and the random placement of the diamonds making up the Star, it was useless to try to get "tasteful" when it came to selecting fabric for the setting squares and triangles. Also, these large squares and triangles were perfect for showcasing the scrumptious large-scale print.

Tradition . . .

Detail of *Pennsylvania Sampler*, c. 1890–1910: While it's not a Lone Star, this single large Star on an open field has a similar feel.

Look Closely: Design Highlights

- Random placement of small diamonds
- Star points stop short of quilt edges
- Star points accentuated with strong fabric frames
- Two fabrics (rather than one) used for framing points
- Bold, large-scale setting fabric

70" × 70" (177.8 cm × 177.8 cm) ▪ 2007

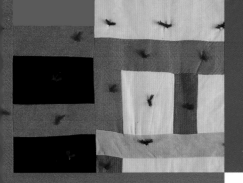

Marzella's Quilt

This is another quilt inspired by the work of an African-American quilter. The original—simply titled *Strips*—was made by Marzella Tatum from Carthage, Texas. We found Marzella's quilt through the same 1998 South Carolina exhibit catalogue where we found Carthage-born Arbie Williams. Must have been something in the water in that town!

From The Parts Department

Strata (page 125)

In addition to the parts, you will need:

- Backing fabric
- Basic tool kit
- Batting
- Binding fabric
- Sashing fabric
- Wool for tying

The design concept for this quilt is very simple, showing that the block doesn't need to be complex to make a bold and successful design. Inspired by the original, we cut up large pieces of various fabrics and separated them, both vertically and horizontally with vibrant red strips, and then created a faux border by doing the same on the left and right sides, substituting turquoise and lime green for the black "chunks" and tossing in a few maverick strips in turquoise, yellow, and purple. The quilt is tied rather than quilted using deep red worsted wool, and we enjoyed the meditative process of tying the many square knots. For the back, we used a lively African print, which you can see peeking over to finish the edges.

Look Closely: Design Highlights

- Variety of black fabrics used for depth and interest
- Rollover binding (back to front)
- Tying as an alternative to quilting
- Try this: Substitute embroidery floss, pearl cotton, or other fibers for wool ties

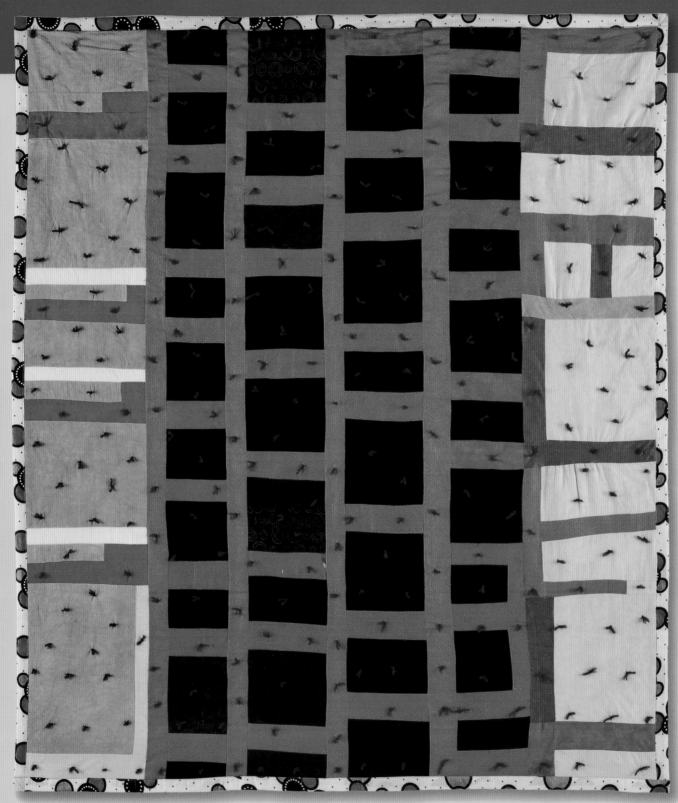

49" × 55" (124.5 cm × 139.7 cm) ▪ 2007

Our Garden

The interplay of the many floral prints, the consistent placement of values, and the recurring rotation of the parts create multiple secondary patterns in this quilt. Every time you look, you see something different. Try it!

From The Parts Department

Our Garden (page 114)

In addition to the parts, you will need:

- Basic tool kit
- Backing fabric
- Batting
- Binding fabric

This quilt was built by relying on an intuitive understanding of the importance of value and the role it plays in defining what we see when we look at our quilts. To create the effect we wanted here, it was necessary to include a sufficient number of dark prints in the large triangles spaced throughout the design. We also decided to use the same black-and-white print consistently in every block to balance out the many busy fabrics.

Once the blocks were sewn together, we agreed that the quilt didn't call for a border. Pieced quilts without borders were common in antique quilts and we think it is still a good option.

Tradition . . .

Detail of *Sampler*, c. 1890–1910: While the fabrics and colors are certainly very different, there are similarities in the arrangement of the large and small triangles between this vintage block and the block in *Our Garden*.

Look Closely: Design Highlights

Sixty-four blocks, each 9" (22.9 cm) square finished

Lots of floral prints to reflect the garden theme

A single print placed consistently in each block maintains order

71" × 71" (180.3 cm × 180.3 cm) ▪ 2006

Pinwheels

This is another of the few quilts we made without a border. We didn't feel it needed one. With so much of the busy print on the outside edges, we created the illusion without the work.

From The Parts Department

Half-Square-Triangle Unit (page 94)
Liberated Log Cabin (page 100)
Pinwheel (page 115)

In addition to the parts, you will need:

- Assorted fabrics for filler strips
- Backing fabric
- Basic tool kit
- Batting
- Binding fabric

This quilt was inspired by the quilts of Gee's Bend, particularly in its use of a busy large-scale print as a key setting element. Each block begins with a pinwheel that is then framed in Liberated Log Cabin style. We made lots of Half-Square-Triangle Units with black-and-white prints and in various sizes to incorporate into the framing strips.

Tradition...

Detail of *Pennsylvania Sampler*, c. 1890–1910: Made with simple half-square triangles, the Pinwheel pattern pops up in many vintage quilts.

Look Closely: Design Highlights

- Nine blocks, each 6" (15.2 cm) square finished
- Some Pinwheel triangles cut from Strata
- Half-Square-Triangle Unit strips used Liberated Log Cabin style
- Wide strips of large-scale paisley play a pivotal role in design

62" × 69" (157.5 cm × 175.3 cm) ▪ 2007

Posies

At first glance, this is a crisp little black-and-white strippy quilt overlaid with colorful flower pots, until you discover the posies for which the piece is named. Freddy made the posies from Yo-Yos, which we hand stitched in place after the quilt was quilted. Some posies are made with a single Yo-Yo; others are two or three layers of different-sized pieces.

From The Parts Department

Bias (Serpentine) Strips (page 84)
Flying Geese (page 90)
Posies (page 116)
Yo-Yo (page 128)

In addition to the parts, you will need:

- Backing fabric
- Basic tool kit
- Batting
- Binding fabric
- Fabric to frame sashing
- Sashing fabric

Having made a number of more traditional Basket quilts, we were ready to return to this alternative, freed-up method of construction. The pots were freehand cut in various shapes, primarily from solid fabrics, and we connected the Yo-Yo posies to the pots with black stems. Serpentine "vines" wander along, adding an extra touch of pizzazz, while rather unruly black-and-white Flying Geese chase each other around the border, changing direction at will to make the perfect finish.

Detail of *Pennsylvania Sampler*, c. 1890–1910: We didn't need to go far to find precedents for the Flying Geese in our *Posies* quilt. Unlike our two-color version, this anonymous quilter was obviously working from her scrap bag. Note the subtle variations in values from goose to goose.

Look Closely: Design Highlights

- Some Yo-Yos face up, some face down
- Stems finish approximately ½" (1.3 cm) wide; serpentine strips finish approximately 1" (2.5 cm) wide
- Pots come in all shapes and sizes
- Not every pot has a posey
- Flying Geese vary in fabric placement and direction
- Posies vary in size; some are a single Yo-Yo, others multiples in various sizes
- Dragonflies in quilting
- Try this: Finish Yo-Yos with buttons or tie them to the quilt with colored yarns or ribbons

38" × 71" (96.5 cm × 180.3 cm) ▪ 2007

Pyramids

Here's a great, traditional one-patch pattern made modern by the choice of fabrics. The single shape is an equilateral (all sides and angles equal) triangle.

From The Parts Department

Pyramid (page 118)

In addition to the parts, you will need:

- Backing fabric
- Basic tool kit
- Batting
- Binding fabric
- Border fabric

This quilt is an example of intuitive designing at its best. We simply cut out a bunch of scrappy triangles in a healthy mix of colors, values, and prints, and then sewed them together into horizontal rows, relying on our instincts for placement. Rather than messing with half-shapes for the ends of the rows, we used full triangles, and then trimmed the side edges of the quilt before adding the border.

The large-scale border fabric was so stunning, and the contrast to the triangle fabrics so great, that it provided the instant "wow" factor we were looking for, as well as a strong frame to keep the interior of the quilt in its place.

Look Closely: Design Highlights

Pyramids cut from a broad range of colors, values, and prints

A great border fabric can make a quilt; change of scale here is key

68" × 80" (172.8 cm × 203.2 cm) ▪ 2006

Ralli Double Serpentine

This quilt features scraps of Ralli (or Snake) quilts made in the villages of Pakistan. We were given these leftovers from an artist friend of Freddy's who includes them in the garments she makes. Look closely and you can see the large running stitches in some of the block centers.

From The Parts Department

Bias (Serpentine) Strips (page 84)
Liberated Log Cabin (page 100)

In addition to the parts, you will need:

- Backing fabric
- Basic tool kit
- Batting
- Binding fabric
- Border fabric

Pakistani Ralli (or Snake) quilts are made from a sandwich of coarsely woven fabric (much like our familiar vintage 1930 feed sacks), a scrap of rayon-type batting, and a pieced backing of totally unrelated fabrics. The quilters sit around a large frame and use a running stitch to secure the layers, working from the outside edges to the center. No two are ever alike, and they all seem to be made in marvelous bright colors. When we were given scraps, we decided that the oddly sized and shaped pieces were ideal for Gwen's Liberated Log Cabin technique, so we "recycled" them in this quilt. The double serpentine border, which we topstitched in place, was a great finishing touch.

Look Closely: Design Highlights

- Liberated techniques are great for mixing fabrics of different textures and weights—no seams to match

- Serpentine strips finish approximately 1" (2.5 cm) wide

- Serpentine strips "soften" what might otherwise be an overpowering border

- Try this: Topstitch serpentine strips with thread in a contrasting color to add another design element

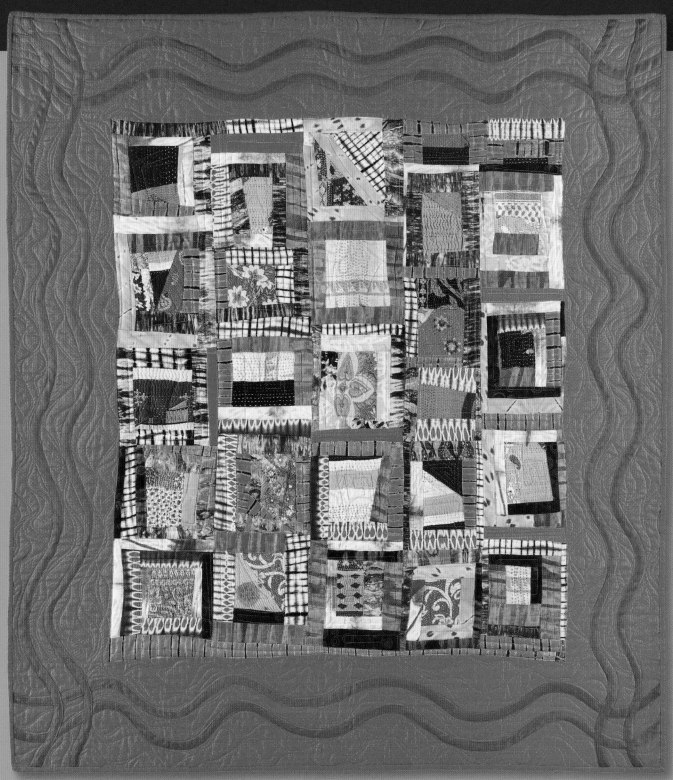

53" × 59" (134.6 cm × 149.9 cm) ▪ 2008

Red and Green Triangles

This very simple quilt—including its pieced border—is made entirely of Half-Square-Triangle Units. As with many antique quilts, it is pieced casually, without concern for sharp points or perfectly matched seams. This very informality is what gives the quilt its undeniable pluck.

From The Parts Department

Half-Square-Triangle Unit (page 94)
Log Cabin Variation II (page 109)

In addition to the parts, you will need:

- Assorted fabrics for border
- Backing fabric
- Basic tool kit
- Batting
- Binding fabric

We love this quilt! Although it employs the simplest of design concepts—the repeating half-square triangle—this playful quilt never fails to fascinate. At first glance it appears uncomplicated, but as you explore more carefully, the whimsical piecing reveals itself and gives the quilt a fresh new appeal. Here again, a golden rule of quilting applied: When triangle units were too small, or when rows came up short, we simply added on. We made no attempt to match the seams from row to row. We believe this is what makes the quilt work artistically. Precisely pieced, it would have been—well—boring.

We added the borders Log-Cabin style, piecing reds and greens unpredictably with florals and geometrics—the perfect finishing touch, we think.

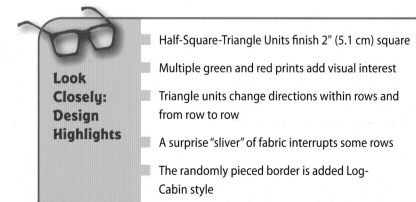

Look Closely: Design Highlights

- Half-Square-Triangle Units finish 2" (5.1 cm) square
- Multiple green and red prints add visual interest
- Triangle units change directions within rows and from row to row
- A surprise "sliver" of fabric interrupts some rows
- The randomly pieced border is added Log-Cabin style

50" × 56" (127.0 cm × 142.2 cm) ▪ 2006

Red Sticks

The blocks around the outside of this quilt are made using the same "part" as the central design. However, by substituting red strips for the many colored inserts in the center area, the blocks create the illusion of a border. It's amazing how this simple modification both shows off and corrals the center design.

From The Parts Department

Sticks (page 124)

In addition to the parts, you will need:

- Backing fabric
- Basic tool kit
- Batting
- Binding fabric

Both of us were dying to do a red quilt, and we were drawn to the idea of inserting narrow strips into blocks of fabric. It is the contrast of the thin, colorful inserts heading off in various directions that makes the design really "pop." We started by cutting same-size pieces of different red fabrics, slicing them up, and adding the inserts, sewing the pieces back together, and trimming up the blocks. We soon realized that the blocks looked more interesting when cut into different lengths, and when we varied the number and the direction of the cuts in each one.

Tradition . . .

Detail of *Four Patch*, c. 1910–1920: This vintage quilt mixes high and low contrast blocks, just as we did in *Red Sticks*. Makes for a more interesting quilt, don't you think?

Look Closely: Design Highlights

- The number and direction of cuts and inserts vary from block to block
- For some blocks, all inserts are cut from the same fabric; in other blocks, we used multiple fabrics
- Some blocks are high contrast, others low contrast
- Monochromatic blocks create the illusion of a border

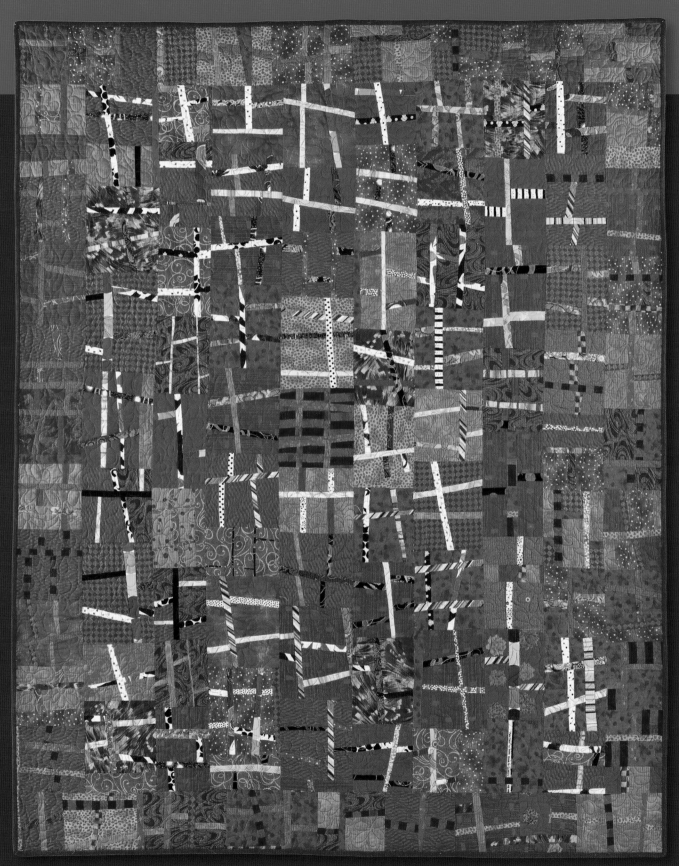

58" × 72" (147.3 cm × 182.9 cm) ▪ 2007

Spider Web

In keeping with the Marston/Moran style for our version of this old favorite, we made nine big blocks in splashy colors, and used black-and-white print corners to define where one block ends and another begins.

From The Parts Department

Spider Web (page 120)

In addition to the parts, you will need:

- Backing fabric
- Basic tool kit
- Batting
- Binding fabric

In her book, *Old Patchwork Quilts and the Women Who Made Them*, first published in 1929 (see Bibliography, page 189), Ruth Finley reminds us that this old-fashioned quilt pattern originated and was named during a time when people tended to spend much more time outdoors than we do today. Spider Web is one of those grand traditional patterns known for its flexibility. Uncomplicated in its construction, it could be made any size and easily accommodates odd-sized scraps.

Look Closely: Design Highlights

Nine large blocks, each finish 20" (50.8 cm) square

Stripes and other directional fabrics add movement to the blocks

Consistent black-and-white print corner squares

58" × 58" (147.3 cm × 147.3 cm) ▪ 2006

Spikes

We *think* we started this quilt as a Chinese Coins design in black, white, and red, with the variation of an occasional elongated Sawtooth element. This is what we ended up with—and we love it!

From The Parts Department

Spike (page 122)

In addition to the parts, you will need:

- Assorted fabrics for filler strips
- Backing fabric
- Basic tool kit
- Batting
- Binding fabric
- Sashing fabric

Many times when we start a quilt with a specific design in mind, it changes without our intention. Rather than considering this a disaster, we simply go with it. In this case, our tricolor Chinese Coins design "strayed" to include Sawtooth (or Spike) elements in varying sizes, orientations, and occasionally colors, with filler strips to keep the rows consistent in width. How much more interesting and vigorous the quilt became! Before we knew it, we were using Strata from The Parts Department for some of the Spikes.

Look Closely: Design Highlights

- The size, shape, and orientation of the Spikes change constantly
- Some Spikes are liberated, others are not
- Some Spikes are cut from Strata instead of a single fabric
- Filler strips balance off-sized parts

54" × 63" (137.2 cm × 160.0 cm) ▪ 2006

What a Star!

This quilt makes a great case for keeping a well-stocked Parts Department. It allows you to come up with so many wonderful design elements that would be impossible to plan in advance.

From The Parts Department

Half-Square-Triangle Unit (page 94)
Liberated Churn Dash (page 96)
Liberated Star (page 104)

In addition to the parts, you will need:

- Assorted fabrics for filler strips
- Backing fabric
- Basic tool kit
- Batting
- Binding fabric
- Border fabric (for on-point setting triangles)
- Two different border fabrics (for unpieced borders)

Here is a wonderful demonstration of how you can update an old favorite. By using the traditional medallion setting, we were able to mix different blocks in varying sizes and sew them together in some sort of recognizable order. The key was to stay flexible. Note the wonky-cut strips around the center Star blocks, the half-Star blocks and filler bits inserted in the borders, and the occasional unexpected brown triangle in the little Sawtooth units.

Tradition . . .

Detail of *Sampler*, c. 1890–1910: Here's the inspiration for Gwen's Liberated Churn Dash blocks. Note the casual placement of the background stripes.

Look Closely: Design Highlights

Mix of some liberated, some traditional blocks in all shapes and sizes

Lots of filler strips—pieced and plain

Split blocks in outer border

A few brown half-square triangles in the Sawtooth borders add the unexpected

73" × 73" (185.4 cm × 185.4 cm) ▪ 2006

About The Authors

Gwen Marston

Gwen Marston is a professional quiltmaker, author, and teacher. She has taught quilting around the world for more than 30 years. She has been a regular columnist in a national quilting magazine for more than a decade. A prolific and respected author, Gwen has written more than 22 books on quilting and was awarded the 2005 Michigan Notable Books award for her tome, *Mary Schafer: American Quilt Maker*.

Her quilts have been shown in many exhibits worldwide. She has had 23 solo exhibits of her work and was honored to have a selection her quilts exhibited by seven museums. She has appeared on numerous television programs, including *Simply Quilts*.

Gwen is serious about continuing the traditions of quilting and for the past 26 years she has offered quilting retreats in the fall for dedicated students of quiltmaking.

When not traveling and teaching, she spends her time creating Liberated quilts on peaceful Beaver Island, Michigan.

Freddy Moran

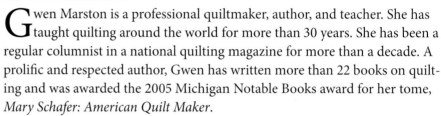

Freddy Moran has been producing her groundbreaking colorful quilts for the past 18 years. Her first quilting book, *Freddy's House*, brought her fearless use of color to a wide audience and is still in demand. Freddy travels and teaches extensively, challenging quilters to break the rules and do what works best for them. She has appeared on national television, including the DIY network. "Red is a neutral" is her quilting mantra.

Freddy lives in Northern California with her husband, Neil. Her five sons and their families continue to keep her busy and fill her with joy.

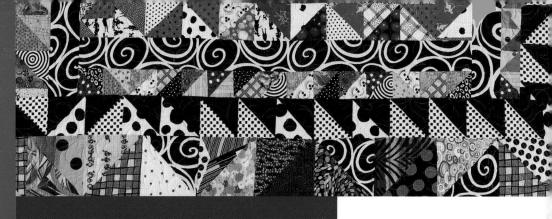

Bibliography

Connecticut Quilt Search Project. *Quilts and Quiltmaking: Covering Connecticut.* Parkesburg, PA: Schiffer Publishing, 2001.

Finley, Ruth E. *Old Patchwork Quilts and the Women Who Made Them.* New York: Grosset & Dunlap, 1929.

Huws, Edrica. *Patchwork Pictures.* Exhibition Catalogue. Japan, 2000.

Leon, Eli. *Who'd a Thought It: Improvisations in African-American Quiltmaking.* San Francisco: San Francisco Craft & Folk Art Museum, 1987.

McClun, Diana, and Laura Nownes. *Quilts! Quilts!! Quilts!!!.* 2nd ed. New York: McGraw-Hill, 1998.

Moran, Freddy, and Gwen Marston. *Collaborative Quilting.* New York: Sterling Publishing Co., Inc., 2006.

Nelson, Cyril I. *The Quilt Engagement Calendar 1992.* New York: E.P. Dutton, 1992.

Vlach, John Michael. *The Afro-American Tradition in Decorative Arts.* Cleveland: The Cleveland Museum of Art, 1978.

Acknowledgments

The collaborative quilts shown in this book were machine quilted by Robyn House, Judy Irish, Kathy Sandbach, and Karen Hanson.

As noted in the captions, Gwen did her own hand quilting. Her machine-quilted quilts were quilted by Robyn House and Jamie Schantz.

We thank our editor, Darra Williamson, for her guidance throughout this process, and Gregory Case, our photographer, for his excellent photography and for being such a joy to work with. To see more of Gregory's work, visit www.gregorycase.com.

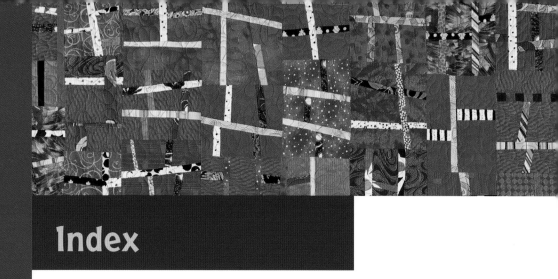

Index